NOTE

1. All recipes serve four unless otherwise stated.

2. All spoon measurements are level.

3. All eggs are sizes 3 or 4 unless otherwise stated.

4. Preparation times given are an average calculated during recipe testing.

5. Metric and imperial measurements have been calculated separately. Use one set of measurements only as they are not exact equivalents.

6. Cooking times may vary slightly depending on the individual oven. Dishes should be placed in the centre of the oven unless otherwise specified.

7. Always preheat the oven or grill to the specified temperature.

8. Spoon measures can be bought in both imperial and metric sizes to give accurate measurement of small quantities.

Delicious Fish Dishes

Delicious Fish Dishes

Mary Morris

TREASURE PRESS

Contents

First published in Great Britain in 1979
in an extended form by Octopus Books Limited under the title
Fish for the Family

Revised edition first published in 1981

This edition published in 1986 by
Treasure Press
59 Grosvenor Street
London W1

Reprinted 1986

ISBN 1 85051 129 2

Printed in Hong Kong

INTRODUCTION

Fish is one of the most important sources of protein in our diet. It is rich in minerals such as calcium, phosphorous and iron, and saltwater fish contain all-important iodine.

Sadly, there is a decline in the number of wet fish shops in the cities, towns and villages because it deprives us of the heads, bones and trimmings, so necessary for fish stock which is the basis of all good fish sauces.

Most of our shopping is now done in the local grocers and supermarkets, which carry a comprehensive range of excellent frozen fish. If there is a fisherman in the family then you are lucky, because there is nothing to compare with fish straight from the sea or river.

Fish is classified into three groups: *white fish*, where the oil is found only in the liver of the fish, e.g. cod, haddock, sole and whiting; *oily fish*, where the oil is dispersed throughout the flesh, e.g. salmon, mackerel, herring and trout; *shellfish*, which are divided into two sections (a) the crustacea, e.g. lobster, crab, crayfish and prawn, and (b) the molluscs, e.g. scallops, mussels, oysters, etc.

All fish are described as round, e.g. mackerel, herring, trout, or flat, e.g. plaice and sole.

Frozen fish may be used throughout this book, following the instructions on the packets.

Choice and purchase of fresh fish

WHITE AND OILY FISH

Really fresh fish is easy to recognize by its bright shining eyes, red gills and firmness of the flesh, with no more than a slight seaweedy smell. Freshwater fish sometimes have a slight muddy smell; soak them in salted water for an hour or two and it will disappear. The flesh of steaks, cutlets and fillets should be close-textured.

Buying whole fish

When buying whole fish, remember that you will lose between 30 and 50 per cent of the total weight after filleting. If you are serving whole cooked fish allow 225 g/8 oz to 350 g/12 oz per person, depending on the type; as a rule the loss will be greater on flat rather than round fish.

SHELLFISH

Shellfish should only be purchased in season (see chart, page 11), alive if possible, but if not, there are certain indications of freshness to look for.

The only smell from shellfish should be of the sea, the eyes of crustacea should be prominent. The tail of a lobster should spring back when stretched, and the claws of a crab should not hang limply when picked up but stay firmly in place.

Crawfish, or langouste, are like large lobsters without the claws, they have firmer flesh and are similar in flavour. Look for the same freshness signs as for lobster.

Prawns, shrimps and crayfish (small river shellfish) should be crisp.

Oysters and mussels should be tightly closed – discard any open ones.

Scallops are frequently sold opened and still attached to the bottom shell, they should have firm, white flesh and a bright orange 'tongue'. Ask the fishmonger for the top shell, clean and scrub it well; it can be used for the service of many foods, not only fish.

Clams, cockles, periwinkles, limpets and whelks should all be intact with unbroken shells and no unpleasant smell.

Preparing fish for cooking

The fishmonger will prepare your fish for cooking, this includes gutting, scaling or skinning, depending on the type. However, it is always useful to know how to do it for yourself.

TO SCALE

All fish have scales, but generally speaking they are only removed by scraping when the skin is to be eaten, as with fried herrings in oatmeal. Soles are skinned before cooking because of their tiny, tough scales. On the other hand, salmon is cooked and the skin removed before eating, so it is very much a question of what you are cooking and how, that decides whether or not it needs to be scaled.

To scale fish, spread newspaper over the working surface as the scales fly everywhere. Using a small sharp knife, scrape the scales from the tail to the head, holding the knife slantwise to the fish.

Always remove the scales before gutting the fish – it is easier.

TO GUT OR CLEAN

It is essential to clean or gut fish thoroughly; carelessly gutted fish will have a bitter flavour and be unwholesome. Use plenty of fresh cold water and handle the fish with care. Once the fish has been emptied a small stiff brush should be used to remove all trace of blood, slime and dark spots. Use a little salt to rub away the black membrane.

Small fish to be served whole can be gutted through the gills. To do this, open under the gills and press out the contents from the middle with your finger and thumb. Wash well.

Larger fish are split open from the gills to half way along the lower half of the body. Remove the contents and reserve the roes if any. Wash the fish and the roes.

For flat fish, cut off the gills and make a small opening behind the head, pull out the inside and wash well.

Eels are skinned before cleaning (see notes on skinning, this page).

Frozen fish are usually cleaned before freezing. The exceptions are red mullet, whitebait and sardines which are never gutted.

Salt fish should be soaked for up to 24 hours in fresh water. Change the water frequently.

Dried fish must also be soaked. Run warm water over it and rub lightly to loosen the flesh and leave to soak for up to 48 hours.

SKINNING AND FILLETING

The method for skinning and filleting varies according to the type of fish. Always work on a board to prevent the fish slipping.

To skin flat fish

To skin a sole, wash the fish and cut off the fins. Make an incision across the base of the tail, push the thumb around the edge of the fish between the skin and the flesh. Holding the fish firmly in one hand, dip the fingers of the other in salt to give a good grip and pull sharply from the tail to the head. Turn over and remove the white skin in the same way.

Plaice is skinned after filleting (see below).

To fillet flat fish

A very sharp pliable knife, preferably a filleting knife, is essential for this. Make an incision following the backbone down the entire length of the fish. Slide the knife under the flesh and remove the fillet with long sweeping strokes. Take the first fillet from the left hand side of the fish (if right-handed), working from the head towards the tail. Turn the fish around and remove the second fillet in the same way, working from the tail to the head. Turn the fish over and repeat the process.

To skin fillets of flat fish

Place the fillet skin side down, and dip your fingers in salt. Holding the tail end, place a sharp knife at an angle of the fish and with a sawing movement detach the flesh from the skin.

To skin round fish

Round fish are skinned from head to tail. Cut a narrow strip from the head to the tail along the spine. Cut through the skin below the head and loosen the skin with the point of a knife, this will give you something to hold on to. Dip your fingers in salt and ease the skin down. Care must be taken to avoid damaging the flesh. Turn the fish over and repeat.

To fillet round fish

Cut off the fins with scissors. Cut down the centre of the back to the bone and cut along the stomach. Remove the flesh from the bones with sweeping strokes. Turn over and remove the second fillet.

Principal methods of cooking fish

Several basic cooking methods are suitable for cooking fish, whether they are whole, filleted or cut into steaks.

POACHING

Most types of whole fish can be cooked in this way. Poaching is cooking in liquid at just below boiling point. It can be done in a fish kettle or a pan on top of the stove or in a fireproof dish in the oven. The fish is put into the cold liquid (court bouillon, water or wine or a combination), brought to the boil, then the heat reduced until the liquid 'shivers'.

Kitchen foil is very useful when poaching; the herbs, seasoning, a little white wine or cider and the fish are wrapped loosely but securely in buttered foil, then covered with cold water. This is brought slowly to the boil, the heat reduced, and poached for the appropriate length of time. This preserves the flavour of the fish and it makes its own sauce.

Timing: This is indicated in the recipes, but remember that cooking time begins from the moment the liquid reaches boiling point.

Gutting a flat fish

Removing the first fillet of fish

Removing the second fillet of fish

Skinning a flat fish

BAKING

Oily fish such as herring, salmon and mackerel are particularly suited to baking; they need very little extra fat as the heat draws out their own. White fish, on the other hand, calls for a lot of butter and constant basting to prevent it from being dry.

Baked fish is often very good with a stuffing. Foil can be used for cooking 'en papillote' (paper parcel cookery). The fish is prepared and wrapped in the same way as for poaching in foil but is baked in a moderate oven without any surrounding liquid in the dish. The parcels can be served straight from the oven to the table, neatly folded back.

FRYING

There are two methods of frying fish; deep fat frying and shallow or butter frying.

Deep fat frying

Fillets of fish and small whole fish are cooked in this way. The perfectly dry fish is dipped in seasoned flour, then beaten egg and finally coated with fresh or dried white breadcrumbs. Alternatively the dry fish can be dipped in batter.

Choose a deep, heavy pan for deep-frying. Sufficient fat must be put in the pan to completely cover the fish, however, the pan should never be more than one-third full of fat.

Pure vegetable oil, clarified dripping or lard are the only fats suitable for deep frying as they are free of water content. Use good quality fat, inferior oils burn easily.

The fat must be at the correct temperature before the fish is fried. The hot fat 'seals' the coating on the fish, thus ensuring a crisp coating on the outside and succulent flesh inside, without any soggy results.

Raise the temperature of the fat in the pan to 185°C to 195°C, 360°F to 380°F according to the thickness of the fish to be cooked. Use a kitchen thermometer to test the temperature. The fat should never smoke, because when it smokes it burns. It should be brought to a blue haze (like the shimmer seen on a hot day). The thicker the fish is the longer it takes to cook and if the fat is too hot, the fish will be browned on the outside before it is cooked through.

Do not try to cook too many pieces of fish at one time, this reduces the heat of the fat and the results will be greasy and soggy instead of crisp and golden. The cooked fish must be drained on soft kitchen paper and, if necessary, kept warm on an uncovered dish in a low oven or under a low grill. When the fat is cold it should be strained before re-using.

SAFETY NOTE
1 *Never fill the fat pan more than one-third.*
2 *Do not leave hot fat unattended. If you are called away, turn off the heat, and if the pan has a handle turn it to the back of the stove.*
3 *Never move a pan of hot fat unless absolutely necessary. Move the pan by lifting; do not drag it.*
4 *If the fat should catch alight, turn off the heat and cover the pan immediately with a lid or asbestos fire blanket.*

Shallow or butter frying

Small round fish, flat fish and fillets of large fish are suitable for shallow frying.

Unlike deep frying, butter or margarine can be used for shallow frying, but it must be clarified first or it will splutter and burn easily. This spluttering is caused by the salt and water content of the fats, which is removed by clarifying. Unclarified butter and oil can be used together, but do not give such a fine flavour.   Dry the fish, dip in seasoned flour, then shake off the surplus, which will burn in the pan.

Heat enough fat to cover the bottom of the pan and cook the coated fish until golden on one side, turn it carefully, using a fish slice, and cook the other side. If the fish is thick, reduce the heat after the initial colouring on both sides and cook gently until done.

GRILLING

Grilling is a suitable method for small whole fish, steaks, cutlets and fillets. The grill must be preheated and the rack well greased or the fish will stick to it and break.

When cooking herring and mackerel, make two or three diagonal cuts through the thickest part of both sides of the fish, to allow the heat to penetrate and the natural oil of the fish to flow. Season the fish with salt and a little freshly ground pepper before cooking. Other than oily fish need to be brushed with melted butter or oil before grilling.

STEAMING

Steamed fish can be delicious. The method is best suited to small fillets, cutlets and thin slices of fish. The fish is laid on a buttered plate, seasoned, covered with a saucepan lid, inverted plate, or buttered greaseproof paper or foil, then placed over a pan of boiling water, which is then reduced to a simmer.

When larger or thick pieces of fish are to be cooked, a proper steamer must be used. Grease the bottom of the steamer or the fish will stick to it.

Cooking shellfish and crustacea

Do not overcook shellfish, it ruins the delicate flavour and toughens the flesh. Wash all shellfish in clear, cold water before cooking.

Lobster

If you are lucky enough to get a live lobster or crab, you are then faced with the unfortunate situation of having to kill it.

There are two ways of killing lobsters:
Method 1: Tie the claws and plunge the lobster, head first, into boiling court bouillon or sea or salted water. Cover the pan, bring back to the boil and simmer for 15 minutes to every 500 g/1 lb. The RSPCA recommend putting the lobster into cold liquid and bringing it to a simmer, this lulls the lobster quietly to its death.
Method 2: Tie the claws. Place the lobster on a board and drive the tip of a very sharp pointed knife through the centre of the cross on the head. This pierces the brain and it dies instantly. Cook as for method 1.

Crab

Proceed as for lobster, method 1. Simmer for 12 minutes to every 500 g/1 lb.

Crawfish

Cook as for lobster.

Dublin bay prawns

Cook as for crayfish, simmering for 10 minutes.

Crayfish

These must be cleaned before cooking. Wash well in cold water, then remove the black intestinal tube under the middle phalanx of the tail. Use the tip of a small knife and your thumb to pull it out. If it breaks the fish will taste bitter. Cook as for lobster, method 1, simmering in salted water or court bouillon for 5 to 8 minutes according to size.

Shrimps

Drop into a large pan of boiling sea or salted water. When it reaches boiling point again, remove from the heat immediately; they are cooked.

Prawns

Cook as for shrimps unless large, then allow 5 minutes simmering time.

Scallops and queens

Open by putting the tightly closed shells in a hot oven for 1 to 2 minutes. Remove from the oven and cut away the beard and black thread. Slide a knife under the fish and remove it from the flat shell, wash and proceed with the chosen recipe.

Oysters

Oysters are best eaten raw, but sometimes they are poached, fried or grilled on skewers. Firstly they must be opened. You need a very short knife with a wide blade. Wrap a kitchen towel around your left hand (if right-handed) and place the oyster flat side up in the palm. Push the knife under the hinge and into the oyster, prizing the two shells apart. Take care not to spill the precious liquid. Serve on the deep shell.

Mussels

Scrub well and pull off the beards from the sides, or scrape off with a small, sharp knife. The beards are very tough and stringy, being the means by which the mussels cling to the rocks. Cook as in the chosen recipe, or proceed as for cockles.

Cockles

Wash in two or three batches of cold water to remove the sand, then leave in a bucket of salted water and they will clean themselves. Place in a large saucepan with just enough water to cover the bottom. Put a folded clean kitchen tea towel or lid over them and shake the pan over fairly high heat until they open.

Whelks

Leave in fresh water for several hours, then drop into boiling salted water. Immediately remove from the heat and leave in the water for an hour to finish cooking. Do not boil whelks or they will become rubbery. Take the whelks out of the shells and remove the hard coverpiece. Serve hot with parsley sauce, or cold with mayonnaise. Alternatively, make into fritters and serve with watercress and brown bread and butter.

Winkles

If you are lucky enough to get some live winkles, wash them well, drop into boiling sea or salted water, bring back to the boil and simmer for 5 minutes. Serve as for whelks.

Availability of fresh fish

Light shaded areas indicate when each fish is available, darker shading indicates when the fish is at its best.

Type	Fish	April	May	June	July	Aug	Sep	Oct	Nov	Dec	Jan	Feb	March
round oily	Anchovy			■	■	■	■						
round white	Bass		░	░	░	░	░						
round white	Bream			░	░	░	░	░	░	░	░	░	░
flat white	Brill	░	░	░									
round white	Carp	░	░	░	░	░	░	░	░	░	░	░	░
round white	Char	░	░	░	░	░	░	░	░	░	░	░	░
shellfish	Cockles	░	░	░	░	░	░			░	░	░	░
round white	Cod	░	░	░	░	░	░	▓	▓	▓	▓	▓	▓
round white	Coley (coalfish, saithe)	░	░	░	░	░	░	░	░	░	░	░	░
round oily	Conger eel	░	░	░	░	░	░						
shellfish	Crab	░	▓	▓	▓	▓	▓	░	░	░	░	░	░
shellfish	Crawfish	░	░	░	░	░	░	░	░	░	░	░	░
shellfish	Crayfish	░	░		░	░	░	░	░	░	░	░	░
flat white	Dab	░	░	░	░	░	░	▓	▓	░	░	░	░
round white	Dace					░	░	░	░	░			
round white	Dory	░	░	░	░	░	░	░	░	░	░	░	░
flat white	Dover sole	░	░	▓	▓	▓	▓	▓	▓	░	░	░	░
shellfish	Dublin Bay prawn	▓	▓	▓	▓	▓	▓	▓	▓	▓	▓	▓	▓
round oily	Eel	░	░		░	░	░	░	░	░	░	░	░
flat white	Flounder	░	░	░	░	░	░	░	░	░	░	░	░
round white	Grey mullet	░	░	░	░	░	░	░	░	░	░	░	░
round white	Gurnard			░	░	░	░	░	░	░	░	░	░
round white	Haddock	░	░	░	░	░	░	▓	▓	▓	▓	▓	░
round white	Hake	░	░	▓	▓	▓	▓	▓	▓	░	░	░	░
flat white	Halibut	░	░			░	░	░	░	░	░	░	░
round oily	Herring	░	░	▓	▓	▓	▓	▓	▓	░	░	░	░
round white	Huss (rock salmon)	░	░	░	░	░	░	░	░	░	░	░	░
flat white	Lemon sole	░	░	░	░	░	░	░	░	░	░	░	░
shellfish	Lobster	▓	▓	▓	▓	▓	▓	░					
round oily	Mackerel	░	░	░	░	░	░	░	░	░	░	░	░
shellfish	Mussel	░	░	░	░	░	░	░	░	░	░	░	░
shellfish	Oyster	░	░	░	░	░	░		░	░	░	░	░
round oily	Pilchard	░	░	░	░	░	░	░	░				
flat white	Plaice		░	░	░	░	░	░	░	░	░	░	░
shellfish	Prawn	░	░	░	░	░	░	░	░	░	░	░	░
shellfish	Queens (small scallops)	░	░	░	░	░	░	░	░	▓	▓	▓	▓
round white	Red mullet		░	░	░	░	░	░	░	░			
round oily	Rainbow trout	░	░	░	░	░	░	░	░	░	░	░	░
round oily	Salmon	░	░	▓	▓	▓	▓						░
round oily	Salmon trout	░	░	▓	▓	▓	▓	░	░	░	░	░	░
shellfish	Scallop	░	░	░	░	░	░	░	▓	▓	▓	▓	▓
round white	Sea bream		░	░	▓	▓	░	░	░	░	░	░	░
shellfish	Shrimp	░	░	░	░	░	░	░	░	░	░	░	░
flat white	Skate	░	░		░	░	░	░	░	░	░	░	░
round oily	Smelt	░	░	░	░	░	░	░	░	░	░	░	░
round oily	Sprat	░	░	░	░	░	░	░	░	░	░	░	░
round oily	Trout	░	░	░	░	░	░						░
flat white	Turbot	░	░	░	░	░	░	░	░	░	░	░	░
shellfish	Whelk	░	░	░	░	░	░	░	░	░	░	░	░
round oily	Whitebait	░	░	░	░	░	░						░
round white	Whiting	░	░	░	░	░	░	░	░	▓	▓	░	░
shellfish	Winkle	░	░	░	░	░	░	░	░	░	░	░	░
flat white	Witch (Torbay sole)	░	░	░	░	░	░	░	░	▓	▓	░	░

⊳● *round white*   ◄● *round oily*   ⋈▷ *flat white*   ℰ *shellfish*
Light shaded areas indicate when each fish is available, darker shading indicates when the fish is at its best.

WHITE FISH

White fish is one of the most easily digested animal foods. This is due to the short fibred flesh and only small amounts of connective tissue and fat. Carefully prepared, cooked and presented it provides interest and variety in our diet. The fish in the majority of the recipes that follow is interchangeable but do remember that a thick cutlet of cod or haddock will take longer to cook than a thin fillet of plaice, so adjust the cooking time accordingly.

The very delicate flavour of white fish calls for careful seasoning, fresh water fish in particular. A squeeze of lemon juice rubbed over cuts in fish will keep it white during cooking, and after cooking a garnish of herb butter adds flavour and colour.

Certain fish have a dry flesh, for example bass, so a rich stuffing or sauce is appropriate. On the other hand plaice has moist flesh and takes well to the grill or frying pan.

Bones can be a hazard and are the chief reason why so much filleted fish is on sale. However, the flavour of fish cooked on the bone is superior and not all bones are lethal, i.e. the cartilaginous fish such as skate, eel and huss or rock salmon as it used to be called.

Simple fish pie

Metric
350 g cooked white fish, flaked
3 hard-boiled eggs, shelled and chopped
4 medium tomatoes, skinned and sliced
2 × 15 ml spoons chopped chives or spring onions
450 ml Bechamel Sauce (page 68)
3 × 15 ml spoons grated Cheddar cheese
3 × 15 ml spoons fresh white breadcrumbs

To garnish:
1 tomato, skinned and sliced
sprig of watercress or parsley

Imperial
12 oz cooked white fish, flaked
3 hard-boiled eggs, shelled and chopped
4 medium tomatoes, skinned and sliced
2 tablespoons chopped chives or spring onions
¾ pint Bechamel Sauce (page 68)
3 tablespoons grated Cheddar cheese
3 tablespoons fresh white breadcrumbs

To garnish:
1 tomato, skinned and sliced
sprig of watercress or parsley

Cooking time: about 15 minutes
Oven: 180°C, 350°F, Gas Mark 4

Arrange the fish, eggs and tomatoes in layers in a lightly buttered ovenproof dish, stir the chives or onion into the well seasoned sauce and pour over the layers in the dish. Mix together the cheese and breadcrumbs and sprinkle on top of the mixture. Bake in a preheated moderate oven for 15 minutes, or until the top is crisp and golden. Garnish with the tomato slices and watercress.

Fish cakes

Metric
350 g cooked white fish,
  flaked
3 medium potatoes, peeled
25 g butter
1 egg, beaten
1 × 15 ml spoon finely
  chopped onion, spring
  onion or shallot
2 × 5 ml spoons tomato
  purée
1 × 15 ml spoon chopped
  fresh parsley
salt
freshly ground black pepper
50 g flour
2 eggs, beaten
100 g dried white
  breadcrumbs
oil or fat for frying
sprig of parsley,
  to garnish

Imperial
12 oz cooked white fish,
  flaked
3 medium potatoes, peeled
1 oz butter
1 egg, beaten
1 tablespoon finely
  chopped onion, spring
  onion or shallot
2 teaspoons tomato
  purée
1 tablespoon chopped
  fresh parsley
salt
freshly ground black pepper
2 oz flour
2 eggs, beaten
4 oz dried white
  breadcrumbs
oil or fat for frying
sprig of parsley,
  to garnish

Simple fish pie; Fish cakes

Cooking time: 20 minutes

Fish cakes are easy to make and, when well-flavoured, excellent to eat. To dry boiled potatoes, strain off the water and place a folded clean teatowel directly on top of the potatoes. Replace the pan on the stove with the heat off, and in 3 to 4 minutes the potatoes will be dry and floury.

Beat the fish well with a wooden spoon in a bowl to break down the fibres. Boil the potatoes, drain, dry and mash, adding the butter, egg, onion, tomato purée, parsley and salt and pepper to taste. Beat in the fish. Using your hands, shape the mixture on a floured board into round cakes. Dip the cakes in beaten egg and coat with the crumbs, pressing them on with a palette knife.

Pour enough oil into a sauté or frying pan to a depth of 1 cm/½ inch. Heat the oil until a breadcrumb browns in it in 30 seconds. Carefully lift in the fish cakes. Fry until coloured, turning once only. Drain on kitchen paper and arrange on a hot serving dish. Garnish with the parsley sprig and serve with tartare sauce.

Plaice colbert

Metric
750 g plaice fillets
juice of ½ lemon
salt
freshly ground black pepper
2 eggs, beaten
100 g fresh white
  breadcrumbs
50 g butter, melted
450 ml Anchovy Sauce
  (page 69)
4 pats Maître d'Hôtel
  Butter (page 78)

Imperial
1½ lb plaice fillets
juice of ½ lemon
salt
freshly ground black pepper
2 eggs, beaten
4 oz fresh white
  breadcrumbs
2 oz butter, melted
¾ pint Anchovy Sauce
  (page 69)
4 pats Maître d'Hôtel
  Butter (page 78)

Cooking time: about 25 minutes
Oven: 190°C, 375°F, Gas Mark 5

Rinse and dry the fillets, sprinkle with the lemon juice and season with salt and pepper. Roll up the length of the fish and dip in beaten egg, then coat in crumbs and secure with a wooden cocktail stick if necessary. Place in a well buttered ovenproof dish, drizzle the melted butter over the fish and bake in a preheated moderately hot oven for 15 to 20 minutes. Place the fish on a hot serving dish, removing the sticks if used. Stir the fish cooking liquid into the anchovy sauce and bring to the boil. Pour round the fish. Garnish with maître d'hôtel butter.

Deep-fried fish fillets

Metric
4 × 175 g fillets of white
  fish, rinsed and skinned
squeeze of lemon juice
salt
300 ml coating batter
50 g flour
freshly ground black pepper
oil or fat for deep frying

Imperial
4 × 6 oz fillets of white
  fish, rinsed and skinned
squeeze of lemon juice
salt
½ pint coating batter
2 oz flour
freshly ground black pepper
oil or fat for deep frying

Cooking time: about 20 minutes

Dry the fish, sprinkle with lemon juice and a little salt. Leave for 20 minutes. Drain away any liquid from the fish, then dry it. Season the flour lightly with salt and pepper. Coat the fish in the flour, shaking off the surplus.
Heat the fat or oil in the pan to 190°C/375°F. Dip the fillets, two at a time, into the batter making sure they are well covered. Lift out and slide carefully into the hot fat. When deep golden and crisp, drain on kitchen paper and keep hot until all the fillets have been fried. Serve with chipped potatoes.

Below: Plaice colbert; Swedish cod bake

Above: Deep-fried fish fillets

Swedish cod bake

Metric
4 × 225 g cod steaks
6 streaky bacon rashers,
  de-rinded
pinch of paprika
salt
freshly ground black pepper
25 g butter
4 small tomatoes
1 garlic clove, peeled and
  crushed
oil
450 ml Mushroom Sauce
  (page 69)
4 sprigs of parsley, to
  garnish

Imperial
4 × 8 oz cod steaks
6 streaky bacon rashers,
  de-rinded
pinch of paprika
salt
freshly ground black pepper
1 oz butter
4 small tomatoes
1 garlic clove, peeled and
  crushed
oil
¾ pint Mushroom Sauce
  (page 69)
4 sprigs of parsley, to
  garnish

Cooking time: about 35 minutes
Oven: 180°C, 350°F, Gas Mark 4

Rinse and dry the fish. Dice the bacon and spread half on the bottom of a lightly buttered ovenproof dish. Lay the fish on top, season with paprika and a little salt and pepper, then cover with the remaining bacon. Dot the butter on top and bake in a preheated moderate oven for 25 to 30 minutes, basting occasionally, until the fish flakes easily.

Meanwhile, rub the whole tomatoes with the crushed garlic, arrange stalk side down in a lightly greased ovenproof dish. Cut crossways on top and brush with a little oil. Bake the tomatoes with the fish during the last 15 minutes of cooking time.

Remove the fish and bacon to a hot serving dish. Add the cooking juices to the mushroom sauce, bring to the boil; then pour into a heated sauce boat. Garnish the fish with the tomatoes and parsley sprigs.

15

The rajah's fish

Metric
750 g white fish fillets
salt
freshly ground black pepper
juice of ½ lemon
3 × 15 ml spoons sweet
  chutney
50 g stoned raisins, chopped
50 g blanched almonds,
  chopped
2 eggs, beaten
100 g fresh white
  breadcrumbs
oil or fat for deep frying
Curried Apricot
  Mayonnaise (page 74),
  to serve

To garnish:
25 g browned, flaked
  almonds
rolled stuffed anchovy
  fillets

Imperial
1½ lb white fish fillets
salt
freshly ground black pepper
juice of ½ lemon
3 tablespoons sweet
  chutney
2 oz stoned raisins, chopped
2 oz blanched almonds,
  chopped
2 eggs, beaten
4 oz fresh white
  breadcrumbs
oil or fat for deep frying
Curried Apricot
  Mayonnaise (page 74),
  to serve

To garnish:
1 oz browned, flaked
  almonds
rolled stuffed anchovy
  fillets

Cooking time: about 20 minutes

Rinse and dry the fillets. Season with salt and pepper and sprinkle with lemon juice. Spread a little chutney on each fillet, cover with some almonds and raisins. Roll up the fillets lengthways, secure with a wooden cocktail stick and dip each fillet in the egg, then coat thoroughly in the crumbs. Heat the oil or fat to 190°C/ 375°F, then fry the fish until golden brown. Drain on kitchen paper. Arrange on a serving dish and garnish with the almonds and anchovy fillets. Serve with curried apricot mayonnaise.

From front: Plaice Veronique; The rajah's fish; Baked stuffed Devon hake

Baked stuffed Devon hake

Metric
1 kg middle cut of hake, bone removed
50 g fresh white breadcrumbs
2 × 5 ml spoons finely chopped fresh parsley
1 × 2.5 ml spoon grated lemon rind
25 g shelled shrimps
1 × 15 ml spoon melted butter
salt
freshly ground pepper
little beaten egg
2 × 15 ml spoons oil
2 × 15 ml spoons browned breadcrumbs
finely sliced rings of green pepper, to garnish
Fresh Tomato Sauce (page 72), to serve

Imperial
2 lb middle cut of hake, bone removed
2 oz fresh white breadcrumbs
2 teaspoons finely chopped fresh parsley
½ teaspoon grated lemon rind
1 oz shelled shrimps
1 tablespoon melted butter
salt
freshly ground pepper
little beaten egg
2 tablespoons oil
2 tablespoons browned breadcrumbs
finely sliced rings of green pepper, to garnish
Fresh Tomato Sauce (page 72), to serve

Cooking time: 30 minutes
Oven: 180°C, 350°F, Gas Mark 4

When time is at a premium you can substitute this home-made filling with a packet of parsley, thyme and lemon stuffing, made up as directed on the packet.

Rinse and dry the fish. In a bowl, mix together the breadcrumbs, parsley, lemon rind, shrimps, melted butter and salt and pepper. Add enough of the egg to bind the mixture. Place the stuffing in the cavity of the fish, then tie around with cotton to keep the shape. Heat the oil in an ovenproof dish and place the fish in it. Baste with the oil and sprinkle with the browned crumbs. Bake in a preheated moderate oven for 25 to 30 minutes. Place the fish on a hot serving dish and remove the cotton. Garnish with the pepper rings and serve with fresh tomato sauce.

Plaice Veronique

Metric
750 g plaice fillets
salt
freshly ground black pepper
250 ml Fish Stock (page 61)
4 × 15 ml spoons dry white wine
2 × 5 ml spoons lemon juice
225 g white grapes
½ lemon

Mornay Sauce:
300 ml Bechamel Sauce (page 68)
1 egg yolk
1 × 15 ml spoon double cream
2 × 15 ml spoons grated Parmesan or Gruyère cheese or a mixture of both
pinch of cayenne
salt
freshly ground black pepper
small clusters of grapes, to garnish (optional)

Imperial
1½ lb plaice fillets
salt
freshly ground black pepper
8 fl oz Fish Stock (page 61)
4 tablespoons dry white wine
2 teaspoons lemon juice
8 oz white grapes
½ lemon

Mornay Sauce:
½ pint Bechamel Sauce (page 68)
1 egg yolk
1 tablespoon double cream
2 tablespoons grated Parmesan or Gruyère cheese or a mixture of both
pinch of cayenne
salt
freshly ground black pepper
small clusters of grapes, to garnish (optional)

Cooking time: 25 minutes
Oven: 180°C, 350°F, Gas Mark 4

Rinse and dry the fillets, then season with salt and pepper. Fold each fillet into three and place in a lightly buttered flameproof dish. Add the fish stock, white wine and lemon juice. Cover with a greased paper and bake in a preheated moderate oven for 20 minutes. Meanwhile, peel (if necessary) and remove the pips from the grapes. Pare the rind from the lemon very thinly and cut into fine shreds. Cook in boiling water for 2 minutes and drain. Remove the pith and membranes from the lemon and cut the flesh into small segments, add to the grapes and heat through in a small pan. Remove the fillets to a hot serving dish, add the grapes and lemon flesh and keep warm. Reduce the fish liquid by boiling, to 2 × 15 ml spoons/2 tablespoons.
Gently heat the bechamel sauce. Lightly beat the egg yolk with the cream, add 2 spoonfuls of the hot sauce, mix well and return to the pan, stirring constantly. Reheat the sauce, do not boil, add the cayenne and the fish liquid. Taste and adjust the seasoning, then pour over the fillets. Garnish with the grapes and lemon shreds.

Fish à la Florentine

Metric
500 g fish fillets: plaice,
brill, halibut or turbot
salt
freshly ground black pepper
50 g butter
1 × 300 g packet frozen leaf
spinach, defrosted
grated nutmeg (optional)
small bunch of spring
onion tops, chopped
100 g button mushrooms,
sliced
450 ml Dutch Sauce
(page 77)

Imperial
1¼ lb fish fillets: plaice,
brill, halibut or turbot
salt
freshly ground black pepper
2 oz butter
1 × 11 oz packet frozen leaf
spinach, defrosted
grated nutmeg (optional)
small bunch of spring
onion tops, chopped
4 oz button mushrooms,
sliced
¾ pint Dutch Sauce
(page 77)

Cooking time: 20 minutes
Oven: 200°C, 400°F, Gas Mark 6

Rinse and skin the fillets. Place them in an ovenproof dish, season with salt and pepper and dot with 25 g/1 oz of the butter. Cover with a buttered paper or foil and cook in a preheated moderately hot oven for 15 minutes.

Squeeze as much moisture as possible out of the spinach. Melt the remaining butter in a small pan, add the spinach and fry, adding a little grated nutmeg if liked. Lay the spinach on the bottom of a hot serving dish and arrange the fish on top. Add the spring onion tops and mushrooms to the Dutch sauce, bring to the boil and cook for 5 minutes. Add the fish liquid and pour the sauce over the fish. Garnish with dill or fennel.

Fish à la Florentine; Grilled halibut Mexicana

Gougère normande

Grilled halibut Mexicana

Metric	Imperial
75 g butter	3 oz butter
2 small onions, peeled and finely chopped	2 small onions, peeled and finely chopped
100 g sliced mushrooms	4 oz sliced mushrooms
2 large tomatoes, skinned, seeded and diced	2 large tomatoes, skinned, seeded and diced
750 g halibut in one piece rinsed, dried and trimmed	1½ lb halibut in one piece, rinsed, dried and trimmed
salt	salt
freshly ground black pepper	freshly ground black pepper
1 tablespoon tomato purée	1 tablespoon tomato purée
3 × 15 ml spoons dry white wine or cider	3 tablespoons dry white wine or cider
1 large avocado pear	1 large avocado pear
fried chopped walnuts, to garnish	fried chopped walnuts, to garnish

Cooking time: about 25 minutes

Melt 50 g/2 oz of the butter in a shallow flameproof dish, add the onion and mushrooms and cook until soft. Add the tomatoes and mix well. Place the fish on top of the mixture and add salt and pepper. Mix the tomato purée and wine together and pour over the fish. Preheat the grill and place the dish under it to lightly brown the fish, then lower the heat to allow it to cook through, basting frequently until the fish flakes easily. Melt the remaining butter in a small pan. Peel, stone and slice the avocado and fry it in the butter until coloured lightly on each side. Carefully remove the skin and bones from the fish, and arrange it on a hot serving dish. Spoon over the hot sauce. Place the avocado slices around the dish and garnish with the walnuts.

Gougère normande

Metric	Imperial
225 g cooked white fish, flaked	8 oz cooked white fish, flaked
50 g peeled prawns, chopped	2 oz peeled prawns, chopped
1 × 200 g can of mussels, drained and quartered	1 × 7 oz can of mussels, drained and quartered
150 ml Bechamel Sauce (page 68)	¼ pint Bechamel Sauce (page 68)
salt	salt
freshly ground black pepper	freshly ground black pepper
1 × 15 ml spoon fresh white breadcrumbs	1 tablespoon fresh white breadcrumbs
1 × 15 ml spoon grated Parmesan cheese	1 tablespoon grated Parmesan cheese
Prince's Sauce (page 72), to serve	Prince's Sauce (page 72), to serve

Choux paste:	Choux paste:
50 g butter	2 oz butter
150 ml water	¼ pint water
65 g plain flour	2½ oz plain flour
2 eggs	2 eggs

Cooking time: 30 minutes
Oven: 200°C, 400°F, Gas Mark 6

To make the choux paste, sift the flour on to a sheet of paper. Bring the water and butter to the boil together in a small pan. When bubbling, draw off the heat and immediately shoot in the flour. Stir until smooth, and the paste leaves the sides of the pan. Do not beat at this stage. Allow the paste to cool slightly.
Whisk the eggs together and gradually add to the paste, beating hard between each addition (this is the way to achieve a light pastry). Keep back a little of the egg if the paste is getting too soft. Lightly grease 4 large scallop shells or individual ovenproof dishes. Pipe or spoon a ring of paste around the edge of each shell.
Mix together the white fish, prawns, mussels and enough of the sauce to bind, then add salt and pepper to taste. Divide the fish mixture between the dishes. Combine the crumbs and cheese and sprinkle over the tops. Bake in a preheated moderately hot oven for 20 to 25 minutes until the pastry is well risen and golden brown. Serve with a green salad and prince's sauce.

Fish mayonnaise Louis

Fish mayonnaise Louis

Metric
175 ml Rémoulade Sauce
  (page 74)
few drops of Tabasco
225 g cold cooked white
  fish, flaked
2 × 15 ml spoons finely
  chopped green pepper
1 × 15 ml spoon finely
  chopped onion
120 ml double cream,
  whipped
salt
freshly ground black pepper
few rinsed and dried leaves
  from a lettuce heart

To garnish:
2 hard-boiled eggs, whites
  cut into strips, yolks
  sieved

Imperial
6 fl oz Rémoulade Sauce
  (page 74)
few drops of Tabasco
8 oz cold cooked white
  fish, flaked
2 tablespoons finely
  chopped green pepper
1 tablespoon finely
  chopped onion
4 fl oz double cream,
  whipped
salt
freshly ground black pepper
few rinsed and dried leaves
  from a lettuce heart

To garnish:
2 hard-boiled eggs, whites
  cut into strips, yolks
  sieved

Fish is particularly good for cold summer food, and any cooked white fish can be used in this recipe.

Mix together the remoulade sauce and Tabasco. Fold in the fish, green pepper, onion, whipped cream and salt and pepper to taste. Arrange the lettuce leaves on 4 individual dishes – scallop shells are ideal. Spoon the mixture into the centre and garnish with the hard-boiled eggs.

Variation:
For a special occasion, replace the white fish with half and half crabmeat and prawns.

Lemon sole en papillottes

Metric
4 × 225 g fillets of lemon
  sole
4 × 15 ml spoons dry
  vermouth
salt
freshly ground black pepper
25 g butter
2 sprigs each of tarragon,
  parsley and chervil,
  finely chopped
4 sprigs of tarragon, to
  garnish

Imperial
4 × 8 oz fillets of lemon
  sole
4 tablespoons dry
  vermouth
salt
freshly ground black pepper
1 oz butter
2 sprigs each of tarragon,
  parsley and chervil,
  finely chopped
4 sprigs of tarragon, to
  garnish

Cooking time: 20 minutes
Oven: 180°C, 350°F, Gas Mark 4

Fish cooked by this method retains all its flavour and juices, making its own natural sauce.

Rinse and dry the fish. Cut 4 pieces of foil large enough to loosely wrap the folded fillets and butter them lightly. Fold the fillets in half and place one in the centre of each foil piece. Sprinkle with vermouth and add salt and pepper. Dot with butter and add the herbs. Wrap loosely, sealing securely. Place on a baking sheet and bake in a preheated moderate oven for 20 minutes. Transfer the parcels to warmed plates and unwrap at the table, taking care not to spill any of the sauce. Garnish with tarragon sprigs. Serve with new potatoes in a smitaine sauce (page 73).

Fish potato puff

Metric	Imperial
225 g cooked fish, flaked	8 oz cooked fish, flaked
225 g mashed, seasoned potatoes	8 oz mashed, seasoned potatoes
2 × 15 ml spoons chopped fresh parsley	2 tablespoons chopped fresh parsley
1 × 5 ml spoon salt	1 teaspoon salt
1 × 15 ml spoon lemon juice	1 tablespoon lemon juice
few drops of Tabasco	few drops of Tabasco
50 g butter	2 oz butter
2 × 15 ml spoons finely chopped celery	2 tablespoons finely chopped celery
1 × 15 ml spoon finely chopped green pepper	1 tablespoon finely chopped green pepper
2 × 5 ml spoons finely chopped onion	2 teaspoons finely chopped onion
3 large eggs, separated	3 large eggs, separated

To garnish:	To garnish:
mustard and cress	mustard and cress
few stuffed green olives, sliced	few stuffed green olives, sliced

Cooking time: 35 minutes
Oven: 180°C, 350°F, Gas Mark 4

In a bowl combine the fish, potatoes, parsley, salt and lemon juice. Add enough Tabasco to season well. Melt the butter in a pan and fry the celery, pepper and onion together until tender. Add to the fish mixture. Stir in the well beaten yolks and whip the mixture with a fork until light.

Beat the egg whites until stiff but not dry and fold them gently but thoroughly into the mixture. Pile the mixture into a lightly greased ovenproof dish and bake in a preheated moderate oven for 30 minutes or until risen and golden brown. Garnish with the mustard and cress and the olive slices.

From front: Lemon sole en papillottes; Fish potato puff

Plaice with quick cucumber sauce

Metric	Imperial
750 g plaice fillets	1½ lb plaice fillets
75 g butter or margarine	3 oz butter or margarine
2 × 15 ml spoons anchovy paste or 3 × 15 ml spoons anchovy essence	2 tablespoons anchovy paste or 3 tablespoons anchovy essence
1 small cucumber, diced	1 small cucumber, diced
1 × 5 ml spoon chopped fresh dill	1 teaspoon chopped fresh dill
1 × 300 ml can condensed mushroom soup	1 × 10 fl oz can condensed mushroom soup
4 × 15 ml spoons plain unsweetened yogurt	4 tablespoons plain unsweetened yogurt
1 tomato, skinned, seeded and chopped	1 tomato, skinned, seeded and chopped
salt	salt
freshly ground black pepper	freshly ground black pepper

Cooking time: 15 minutes

If you dislike the 'gluey' quality of plaice skin, remove it as described in the notes on skinning, page 8.

Rinse the fillets and dry them well. Melt the butter in a frying pan, add the anchovy paste or essence and fillets, then fry over a medium heat until the fish is golden, turning once only. In a bowl combine the remaining ingredients, add salt and pepper to taste and spoon over the fish. Cover the pan and heat through gently for about 5 minutes. Remove the fillets to a warm serving dish and pour over the sauce.

Aberdeen whiting

Metric	Imperial
4 small whiting, cleaned	4 small whiting, cleaned
2 × 15 ml spoons flour	2 tablespoons flour
50 g butter	2 oz butter
2 × 15 ml spoons chopped fresh parsley	2 tablespoons chopped fresh parsley
2 × 15 ml spoons chopped spring onion	2 tablespoons chopped spring onion
150 ml milk	¼ pint milk
2 × 15 ml spoons double cream	2 tablespoons double cream
salt	salt
freshly ground black pepper	freshly ground black pepper
4 lemon butterflies, to garnish	4 lemon butterflies, to garnish

Cooking time: 15 minutes

This very simple and delicious recipe needs careful cooking. The fish must be cooked gently or it will break up.

Rinse the fish and dry them. Coat in flour, shaking off the surplus. Melt the butter in a large frying pan, add the fish and cook gently for 5 minutes on each side. Mix the parsley, spring onion, milk and cream together and add salt and pepper to taste. Pour the sauce over the fish and cook for another 5 minutes. Transfer the fish to a warm serving dish and pour over the sauce. Garnish with the lemon butterflies.

Halibut in orange herb sauce

Metric
1 kg halibut, cut into four
  steaks
900 ml cold Fish Stock
  (page 61)
1 small onion, peeled and
  finely chopped
15 g butter
2 × 5 ml spoons oil
175 ml frozen concentrated
  orange juice
2 × 5 ml spoons chopped
  fresh tarragon
2 × 5 ml spoons chopped
  fresh parsley
salt
freshly ground black pepper
2 × 5 ml spoons cornflour
1 × 15 ml spoon water
150 ml soured cream

To garnish:
8 orange segments, cleaned
  of pith and membrane

Imperial
2 lb halibut, cut into four
  steaks
1½ pints cold Fish Stock
  (page 61)
1 small onion, peeled and
  finely chopped
½ oz butter
2 teaspoons oil
6 fl oz frozen concentrated
  orange juice
2 teaspoons chopped
  fresh tarragon
2 teaspoons chopped
  fresh parsley
salt
freshly ground black pepper
2 teaspoons cornflour
1 tablespoon water
¼ pint soured cream

To garnish:
8 orange segments, cleaned
  of pith and membrane

From left: Plaice with quick cucumber sauce; Aberdeen
whiting; Halibut in orange herb sauce

Cooking time: about 30 minutes

Brill is a good substitute for halibut, but any white fish
can be cooked in this way.

Rinse the fish and dry it. Trim off any fins, then
place in a lightly buttered flameproof dish. Pour over
the fish stock, bring to the boil, reduce the heat immediately and poach for 10 minutes. Remove the
fish from the liquid on to a warm serving dish,
remove skin and bones and keep hot. Strain off 150 ml/
¼ pint of the liquid and reserve.

Fry the onion gently in the butter and oil, stir in the
orange juice, reserved fish liquid, herbs and salt and
pepper to taste. Bring to the boil and simmer for 3
minutes. Mix the cornflour with the water, stir into the
sauce, bring slowly to the boil, stirring constantly.
Remove from the heat and stir in the soured cream.
Taste and adjust the seasoning, then pour the sauce
over the steaks and garnish with orange segments.

Cod niçoise; Paprika fish

Cod niçoise

Metric
4 × 225 g cod fillets, skinned
salt
freshly ground black pepper
150 ml dry white wine
150 ml water
slice of onion
bouquet garni
1 garlic clove, peeled and
    crushed
40 g butter
40 g flour
150 ml milk
1 × 15 ml spoon double
    cream
2 large tomatoes
    skinned, seeded and diced
1 green pepper, cored,
    seeded and finely
    chopped

To garnish:
12 black olives, pitted
1 × 15 ml spoon chopped
    fresh parsley

Imperial
4 × 8 oz cod fillets, skinned
salt
freshly ground black pepper
$\frac{1}{4}$ pint dry white wine
$\frac{1}{4}$ pint water
slice of onion
bouquet garni
1 garlic clove, peeled and
    crushed
$1\frac{1}{2}$ oz butter
$1\frac{1}{2}$ oz flour
$\frac{1}{4}$ pint milk
1 tablespoon double
    cream
2 large tomatoes
    skinned, seeded and diced
1 green pepper, cored,
    seeded and finely
    chopped

To garnish:
12 black olives, pitted
1 tablespoon chopped
    fresh parsley

Cooking time: 30 minutes
Oven: 180°C, 350°F, Gas Mark 4

Rinse and dry the fillets, lay them in an ovenproof dish and add salt and pepper. Pour over the wine and water, adding the onion, bouquet garni and garlic. Cover with buttered greaseproof paper and poach in a preheated moderate oven for 20 minutes. Drain off and reserve the liquid, keep the fish hot on a serving dish.

Melt the butter in a small pan and stir in the flour, cook for 1 minute. Remove from the heat and gradually stir in 300 ml/$\frac{1}{2}$ pint of the reserved fish liquid. Return the pan to the heat and bring to the boil, stirring, until the sauce is thick and smooth. Simmer for 2–3 minutes. Stir in the milk and cream, then taste and adjust the seasoning. Add the tomato and green pepper and reheat to boiling. Pour the sauce over the fish. Garnish with the olives and parsley.

Paprika fish

Metric	Imperial
4 × 225 g witch or lemon sole fillets	4 × 8 oz witch or lemon sole fillets
40 g butter	1½ oz butter
2 medium onions, peeled and finely sliced	2 medium onions, peeled and finely sliced
juice of ½ lemon	juice of ½ lemon
150 ml double cream	¼ pint double cream
1 × 15 ml spoon paprika	1 tablespoon paprika
1 × 5 ml spoon tomato purée	1 teaspoon tomato purée
salt	salt
freshly ground black pepper	freshly ground black pepper

To garnish:

Metric	Imperial
1 cap of canned pimento, finely sliced	1 cap of canned pimento, finely sliced
1 × 15 ml spoon chopped fresh parsley	1 tablespoon chopped fresh parsley

Cooking time: about 25 minutes
Oven: 180°C, 350°F, Gas Mark 4

Rinse the fillets, pat dry, and fold them in half. Melt the butter in a pan, add the onions and fry them until soft and beginning to colour. Spread the onions in an ovenproof dish and lay the folded fillets on top. Sprinkle with lemon juice.

Beat the cream lightly with the paprika, tomato purée and salt and pepper to taste. Pour the mixture over the fish and bake in a preheated moderate oven for 15 minutes, basting with the sauce at intervals. Remove the fish to a hot serving dish, pour over the sauce and garnish with a lattice of the sliced pimento and sprinkle with parsley.

Bream à l'Indienne

Metric	Imperial
75 g butter	3 oz butter
100 g onions, peeled and finely chopped	4 oz onions, peeled and finely chopped
2 × 5 ml spoons curry powder	2 teaspoons curry powder
1 garlic clove, peeled and crushed	1 garlic clove, peeled and crushed
750 g bream fillets	1½ lb bream fillets
salt	salt
freshly ground black pepper	freshly ground black pepper
4 tomatoes, skinned, seeded and roughly chopped	4 tomatoes, skinned, seeded and roughly chopped
250 ml dry white wine	8 fl oz dry white wine
120 ml double cream	4 fl oz double cream

To garnish:

Metric	Imperial
salted peanuts	salted peanuts
sprig of watercress	sprig of watercress

Cooking time: about 35 minutes
Oven: 180°C, 350°F, Gas Mark 4

Melt 50 g/2 oz of the butter in a saucepan, add the onions and cook until softened. Add the curry powder and garlic and cook for 2 to 3 minutes. Season the fillets with salt and pepper and place them in a buttered ovenproof dish. Spread the onion mixture over the fish, add the tomatoes, dot with the remaining butter and pour over the wine. Bake in a preheated moderate oven for 12 minutes, basting frequently. Add the cream and continue to baste at intervals until the fish is cooked, about 20 minutes altogether. Dish the fish, boil the sauce to thicken it, then pour over the fish. Garnish with peanuts and watercress.

Bream à l'Indienne

Plaice à la meunière

Metric	Imperial
750 g plaice fillets	1½ lb plaice fillets
100 g flour	4 oz flour
salt	salt
freshly ground black pepper	freshly ground black pepper
120 ml milk	4 fl oz milk
175 g butter	6 oz butter
juice of ½ lemon	juice of ½ lemon
2 × 15 ml spoons chopped fresh parsley	2 tablespoons chopped fresh parsley
1 lemon, quartered, to garnish	1 lemon, quartered, to garnish

Cooking time: about 25 minutes

Butter is essential to the flavour of this dish. Take care not to overheat the pan, as butter burns very easily.

Rinse and dry the fillets. Season the flour well with salt and pepper. Dip the fillets in the milk, drain, then coat in the flour, shaking off the surplus. Melt 100 g/4 oz of the butter in a large pan and fry the fillets carefully until golden on both sides.

Place the fish on a hot serving dish and keep warm. Wipe out the pan. Melt the remaining butter in the pan and allow to cook to a golden brown. Immediately add the lemon juice and parsley, and taste and adjust the seasoning. Pour the juices over the fish and garnish with lemon wedges.

From front: Plaice à la meunière; Fish Creole;
Rousette sauce tomate

Rousette
sauce tomate

Metric
750 g huss, cut into short
    lengths
50 g flour
salt
freshly ground black pepper
4 × 15 ml spoons olive oil
    or 75 g butter
500 g ripe tomatoes,
    skinned, seeded and diced
3 garlic cloves, peeled and
    crushed
1 × 15 ml spoon chopped
    fresh basil or marjoram
    or 1 × 5 ml spoon dried
1 × 15 ml spoon chopped
    fresh parsley
salt
freshly ground pepper

To garnish:
12 black olives, pitted
fried bread croûtons

Imperial
1½ lb huss, cut into short
    lengths
2 oz flour
salt
freshly ground black pepper
4 tablespoons olive oil
    or 3 oz butter
1 lb ripe tomatoes,
    skinned, seeded and diced
3 garlic cloves, peeled and
    crushed
1 tablespoon chopped
    fresh basil or marjoram
    or 1 teaspoon dried
1 tablespoon chopped
    fresh parsley
salt
freshly ground pepper

To garnish:
12 black olives, pitted
fried bread croûtons

Cooking time: about 15 minutes

Roussette (huss or rock salmon) has firm tasty flesh
and the advantage of being reasonable in price. It is
always cleaned and skinned at the fishmongers. Use
olive oil for the best results, rather than butter.

Rinse and dry the fish. Season the flour with salt and
pepper and coat the fillets with it, shaking off the
surplus. Heat 2 × 15 ml spoons/2 tablespoons of the
oil or 50 g/2 oz of the butter in a frying pan and
fry the fish gently, turning once, until golden. In
another pan, heat the remaining oil or butter and add
the tomatoes, garlic, herbs, and salt and pepper to taste.
Cook gently for 5 minutes. Arrange the fish on a hot
serving dish and spread the sauce over. Garnish with
the olives and croûtons.

Fish Creole

Metric
1 kg cod or fresh haddock
    fillets
25 g butter or margarine
1 medium onion, peeled and
    chopped
2 × 15 ml spoons chopped
    green pepper
1 celery stick, chopped
1 × 400 ml can tomatoes,
    chopped
1 × 2.5 ml spoon chopped
    fresh thyme or marjoram
1 garlic clove, peeled and
    crushed
1 × 15 ml spoon sugar
salt
freshly ground black pepper

Imperial
2 lb cod or fresh haddock
    fillets
1 oz butter or margarine
1 medium onion, peeled and
    chopped
2 tablespoons chopped
    green pepper
1 celery stick, chopped
1 × 14 fl oz can tomatoes,
    chopped
½ teaspoon chopped
    fresh thyme or marjoram
1 garlic clove, peeled and
    crushed
1 tablespoon sugar
salt
freshly ground black pepper

To garnish:
50 g peeled shrimps
4 sprigs of watercress

To garnish:
2 oz peeled shrimps
4 sprigs of watercress

Cooking time: about 25 minutes
Oven: 160°C, 325°F, Gas Mark 3

Rinse and dry the fillets, then arrange in a lightly
buttered ovenproof dish. Melt the butter in a saucepan,
add the onion, pepper and celery and cook until tender.
Add the tomatoes and enough of their liquid to
moisten well. Stir in the thyme or marjoram, garlic,
sugar and salt and pepper to taste. Pour the tomato
mixture over the fillets and bake in a preheated
moderate oven for 20 minutes or until the fish flakes
easily. Garnish with shrimps and watercress sprigs.

OILY FISH

The fat content of fish is dispersed among the flesh and the amount differs according to type and time of year. This dictates the 'seasons', which can be seen on the chart of availability of all types of fish on page 11.

During the spring and autumn the herring is spawning: the fat is used up and the fish get thin, so although the herring is available all year the time to enjoy it at its finest is the summer. The salmon is at its best when it leaves the sea to travel up the river to its spawning ground. It is only at this time that the white milky curd is to be found between the flakes. Once the salmon leaves the sea it eats nothing until its return – living as it does off its own fat.

The trout is a member of the salmon family and is divided roughly into two classes, migratory, i.e. salmon trout, and non-migratory, i.e. lake and river trout. The former are cooked as for salmon while the latter lend themselves to many different methods. The colour of the flesh varies between white and pink and has a very delicate flavour.

Sardines are really young pilchards, however Norwegian sardines are sprats and American sardines are young herrings.

Fish with a high fat content are more difficult to digest and the use of breadcrumbs or oatmeal coatings are recommended.

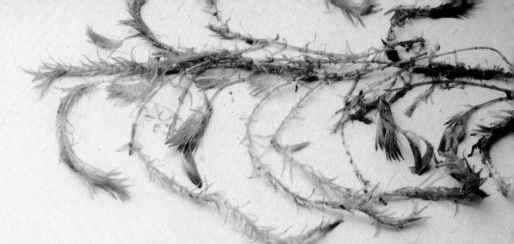

Salmon and pickle loaf

Metric
500 g cold cooked salmon, flaked
50 g fresh white breadcrumbs
150 ml milk
50 g gherkins, coarsely chopped
2 eggs, beaten
1 × 15 ml spoon melted butter
salt
freshly ground black pepper
squeeze of lemon juice
2 × 5 ml spoons very finely chopped onion
300 ml Bechamel Sauce (page 68)

To garnish:
1 hard-boiled egg, white chopped, yolk sieved
6 stuffed olives, sliced

Imperial
1 lb cold cooked salmon, flaked
2 oz fresh white breadcrumbs
¼ pint milk
2 oz gherkins, coarsely chopped
2 eggs, beaten
1 tablespoon melted butter
salt
freshly ground black pepper
squeeze of lemon juice
2 teaspoons very finely chopped onion
½ pint Bechamel Sauce (page 68)

To garnish:
1 hard-boiled egg, white chopped, yolk sieved
6 stuffed olives, sliced

Cooking time: 55 minutes
Oven: 180°C, 350°F, Gas Mark 4

Mix together the salmon, breadcrumbs, milk, gherkins, eggs and melted butter. Add salt, pepper and lemon juice to taste. Pack into a well greased 15 cm/6 inch soufflé dish. Stand the dish in a baking tin, half filled with hot water, and bake in a pre-heated moderate oven for 40 minutes, or until firm to the touch. Turn the fish out on to a hot serving dish and keep warm.
Stir the onion into the sauce, bring to the boil and simmer for 3 minutes. Taste and adjust seasoning. Garnish the loaf with egg and olives, and serve the sauce separately.

Soused herrings

Metric
4 herrings, scaled and cleaned
300 ml dry white wine
150 ml white wine vinegar
1 carrot, peeled and finely sliced
1 onion, peeled and finely sliced
bouquet garni
6 peppercorns
2 bay leaves
2 cloves
3 mace blades
1 × 2.5 ml spoon whole allspice
salt
1 × 15 ml spoon olive or vegetable oil

Imperial
4 herrings, scaled and cleaned
½ pint dry white wine
¼ pint white wine vinegar
1 carrot, peeled and finely sliced
1 onion, peeled and finely sliced
bouquet garni
6 peppercorns
2 bay leaves
2 cloves
3 mace blades
½ teaspoon whole allspice
salt
1 tablespoon olive or vegetable oil

Cooking time: about 30 minutes
Oven: 180°C, 350°F, Gas Mark 4

A souse is used to preserve, tenderize and flavour, its acidity being particularly good with oily fish. It is rather harsh when made with malt vinegar, but less so using half wine vinegar and water.

Rinse the herrings, then place the roes back inside. Pour the wine and vinegar into a pan and add the carrot, onion, bouquet garni, peppercorns, bay leaves, cloves, mace, allspice and a little salt. Bring to the boil and simmer until the vegetables are cooked. Taste and adjust the seasoning. Arrange the fish in an oven-proof dish and pour the hot souse over them. Pour the oil over the top and poach in a preheated moderate oven for 15 minutes. Allow the fish to cool in the liquid, then serve from the dish or refrigerate over-night.

Variations:
Small mackerel or trout may be used in place of the herrings.

Soused herrings; Salmon and pickle loaf

Herring roe pâté

Metric
175 g soft herring roes
4 × 15 ml spoons dry
   white wine
1 onion, peeled and
   sliced
75–100 g butter, softened
cayenne pepper
salt
freshly ground black pepper
2 × 15 ml spoons lemon
   juice
2 × 5 ml spoons chopped
   fresh dill
salted almonds, to garnish

Imperial
6 oz soft herring roes
4 tablespoons dry
   white wine
1 onion, peeled and
   sliced
3–4 oz butter, softened
cayenne pepper
salt
freshly ground black pepper
2 tablespoons lemon
   juice
2 teaspoons chopped
   fresh dill
salted almonds, to garnish

Cooking time: 8 to 10 minutes

Rinse the roes, trim them to remove any membrane, if necessary, then drain on kitchen paper. Pour the wine into a small pan, add the onion and bring to the boil. Remove from the heat, place the roes carefully in the pan, return to the heat, cover and poach for 3 minutes. Take out the roes and allow to cool.

Uncover the pan and reduce the wine by boiling rapidly to 2 × 5 ml spoons/2 teaspoons. Sieve the roes and mix into the butter. Strain in the wine. Mix well together, then add cayenne and salt and pepper to taste. Add the lemon juice and dill. Spoon into cocottes or small individual dishes and chill lightly. Garnish with almonds and dill or fennel fronds. Serve with fingers of toast or any crispbread.

Variation:
Mackerel roes may be used instead of the herring.

Herring roe pâté

Fried whitebait; Cod's roe St. Annes

Fried whitebait

Metric	Imperial
500 g whitebait	1 lb whitebait
100 g flour	4 oz flour
salt	salt
freshly ground black pepper	freshly ground black pepper
oil for deep frying	oil for deep frying
To garnish:	To garnish:
1 lemon, quartered	1 lemon, quartered
few sprigs of parsley	few sprigs of parsley

Cooking time: 12 to 15 minutes

Pick over the whitebait, discarding any crushed or broken ones. If it is necessary to wash the fish, use ice cold water and carefully pat them as dry as possible on a tea towel.

Spread the flour on a sheet of paper and season with salt and pepper. Heat the oil to 190°C/375°F. Take a quarter of the fish and toss them in the flour, making sure they are well covered. Transfer them to the frying basket and shake off any surplus flour. Plunge the basket into the oil for 2 minutes. Drain the fish on kitchen paper and fry the remaining three batches.

When all the fish is cooked check the oil temperature and tip all the whitebait into the frying basket. Plunge the basket into the oil to re-heat and crisp the fish, about 2 minutes. Drain the fish on kitchen paper, then pile them on to a serving dish and garnish with lemon quarters and parsley. Serve very thin brown bread and butter separately.

Cod's roe St. Annes

Metric	Imperial
1 hard cod's roe (about 500 g)	1 hard cod's roe (about 1 lb)
salt	salt
freshly ground black pepper	freshly ground black pepper
2 eggs, beaten	2 eggs, beaten
100 g fresh white breadcrumbs or medium oatmeal	4 oz fresh white breadcrumbs or medium oatmeal
oil for shallow frying	oil for shallow frying
8 streaky bacon rashers, de-rinded	8 streaky bacon rashers, de-rinded
tomato wedges, to garnish	tomato wedges, to garnish
Fresh Tomato Sauce (page 72), to serve	Fresh Tomato Sauce (page 72), to serve

Cooking time: 25 minutes

Canned hard cod's roe can be used if the fresh variety is unobtainable.

Wipe the roe with a damp cloth and tie it in muslin. Simmer in slightly salted water for 10 to 15 minutes, according to thickness. Drain, remove the muslin and cool the roe. Carefully strip off the skin and cut the roe into 8 slices. Season with salt and pepper, dip in egg and coat in breadcrumbs or oatmeal. Pour enough oil into a pan to cover a depth of 10 mm/$\frac{1}{2}$ inch. When hot, fry the roe slices, turning once, until lightly golden. Drain on kitchen paper. Grill or fry the rashers, then roll them up and secure with wooden cocktail sticks. Arrange the roe slices on a hot serving dish and place a bacon roll on top of each one. Garnish with tomato wedges and serve fresh tomato sauce separately.

31

Tuna Madras

Metric
4 × 175 g slices of
  fresh tunny
freshly ground black pepper
1 × 15 ml spoon olive oil
1 × 50 g can anchovy fillets
1 × 15 ml spoon flour
300 ml light chicken stock
1 × 5 ml spoon curry paste
2 bananas
50 g butter
chopped fresh coriander
  leaves or parsley, to
  garnish

Imperial
4 × 6 oz slices of
  fresh tunny
freshly ground black pepper
1 tablespoon olive oil
1 × 2 oz can anchovy fillets
1 tablespoon flour
½ pint light chicken stock
1 teaspoon curry paste
2 bananas
2 oz butter
chopped fresh coriander
  leaves or parsley, to
  garnish

Cooking time: about 40 minutes
Oven: 190°C, 375°F, Gas Mark 5

Rinse and dry the fish, then lay them in a shallow baking tin. Season with pepper and pour over the oil. Arrange half the anchovies over the fish slices, cover with oiled greaseproof paper and bake in a preheated moderately hot oven for 25 minutes.

Meanwhile peel and slice the bananas diagonally, then fry lightly in the butter for about 3 minutes. Keep warm. Arrange the fish on a hot serving dish and keep warm.

Stir the flour into the baking tin, then cook on top of the stove, stirring, for 2 to 3 minutes. Gradually stir in the stock and cook until the sauce thickens. Add the curry paste and cook for a further 5 minutes. Pour the sauce over the fish and sprinkle with coriander or parsley. Arrange the remaining anchovy fillets on top, and surround with the bananas.

Mediterranean mackerel fillets

Metric
4 mackerel, cleaned and
  filleted
salt
freshly ground pepper
50 g flour
4 × 15 ml spoons olive oil
100 g shallots or onions,
  peeled and finely
  chopped
3 garlic cloves, peeled and
  crushed
1 × 15 ml spoon of wine
  vinegar

To garnish:
cooked French beans
1 lemon, quartered

Imperial
4 mackerel, cleaned and
  filleted
salt
freshly ground pepper
2 oz flour
4 tablespoons olive oil
4 oz shallots or onions,
  peeled and finely
  chopped
3 garlic cloves, peeled and
  crushed
1 tablespoon wine
  vinegar

To garnish:
cooked French beans
1 lemon, quartered

Cooking time: 25 minutes

Olive oil is essential for the authentic flavour of this simple but good dish.

Rinse and dry the fillets. Season the flour with salt and pepper and coat the fillets in the flour, shaking off the surplus. Heat 3×15 ml spoons/3 tablespoons of the oil in a large frying pan and fry the fish until golden brown on each side. Drain the fish, then arrange on a hot serving dish. Keep warm.

Heat the remaining oil in a small pan and gently fry the shallots or onions and garlic, until soft. Add the vinegar, taste and adjust the seasoning and pour over the fish. Garnish with the beans, cut into diamonds, and the lemon quarters.

Mediterranean mackerel fillets; Tuna Madras

Stuffed baked herrings

Cooking time: 30 minutes
Oven: 180°C, 350°F, Gas Mark 4

Metric
4 herrings with soft roes
3 × 15 ml spoons grated
  eating apple
1 × 15 ml spoon grated
  onion
1 × 15 ml spoon chopped
  fresh parsley
grated rind of ½ lemon
salt
freshly ground black pepper
25 g butter
1 egg yolk, beaten
2 × 15 ml spoons coarse
  oatmeal
sprig of parsley, to garnish
150 ml Apple and
  Horseradish Sauce
  (page 71), to serve

Imperial
4 herrings with soft roes
3 tablespoons grated
  eating apple
1 tablespoon grated
  onion
1 tablespoon chopped
  fresh parsley
grated rind of ½ lemon
salt
freshly ground black pepper
1 oz butter
1 egg yolk, beaten
2 tablespoons coarse
  oatmeal
sprig of parsley, to garnish
¼ pint Apple and
  Horseradish Sauce
  (page 71), to serve

Scale, clean, bone, rinse and dry the fish. Cut the roes into 2.5 cm/1 inch pieces. Mix together the grated apple, onion, parsley, lemon rind and roes, add salt and pepper to taste and fry gently in 15 g/½ oz of the butter for 3 minutes. Remove from the heat, then stuff the herrings with the mixture. Place the fish in a greased ovenproof dish, brush with the egg yolk and sprinkle with oatmeal. Dot with the remaining butter and bake in a preheated moderate oven for 30 minutes. Garnish with parsley and serve with the sauce.

From left: Stuffed baked herrings; Victoria herrings; Mackerel with gooseberry cream

Victoria herrings

Metric	Imperial
4 herrings, scaled and cleaned	4 herrings, scaled and cleaned
oil for brushing	oil for brushing
salt	salt
freshly ground black pepper	freshly ground black pepper
1 × 5 ml spoons mustard powder	1 teaspoon mustard powder
2 × 15 ml spoons white wine vinegar	2 tablespoons white wine vinegar
300 ml Bechamel Sauce (page 68)	½ pint Bechamel Sauce (page 68)
1–1½ × 5 ml spoons anchovy essence	1–1½ teaspoons anchovy essence
1 × 2.5 ml spoon dried tarragon	½ teaspoon dried tarragon
pinch of cayenne pepper	pinch of cayenne pepper

To garnish:
4 tomato halves, grilled
sprig of watercress

To garnish:
4 tomato halves, grilled
sprig of watercress

Cooking time: 15 minutes

Rinse the fish. Remove any soft roes and keep on one side. Slash the fish diagonally in 3 places on each side and brush with oil. Grill under a high heat for about 8 minutes, turning once. Season with salt and pepper as they open up. Arrange the fish on a hot serving dish and keep warm.

Mix the mustard with the vinegar and add to the bechamel sauce. Stir in the anchovy essence. Cut up the soft roes and add to the sauce together with the tarragon and cayenne. Simmer together for 4 to 5 minutes. Taste and adjust the seasoning. Garnish the fish with the tomato halves and watercress and serve the sauce separately.

Mackerel with gooseberry cream

Metric	Imperial
4 × 175 g mackerel, backbone removed	4 × 6 oz mackerel, backbone removed
50 g fresh breadcrumbs	2 oz fresh breadcrumbs
3 × 15 ml spoons chopped watercress	3 tablespoons chopped watercress
90 g butter, softened	3½ oz butter, softened
salt	salt
freshly ground black pepper	freshly ground black pepper
1 × 425 g can of gooseberries	1 × 15 oz can of gooseberries
50 g sugar	2 oz sugar
sprigs of watercress, to garnish	sprigs of watercress, to garnish

Cooking time: 35 minutes
Oven: 190°C, 375°F, Gas Mark 5

Rinse and dry the fish. Add the breadcrumbs and watercress to 75 g/3 oz of the butter and season well with salt and pepper. Stuff the fish with the mixture. Place the fish in a lightly greased ovenproof dish, cover with foil and bake in a preheated moderately hot oven for 30 minutes.

Rub the gooseberries through a sieve, or liquidize with their syrup, heat in a small pan with the sugar and remaining butter. Pour over the fish and garnish with watercress. Serve with potato croquettes.

Trout with almonds

Metric
4 × 175 g trout, cleaned
4 × 15 ml spoons milk
50 g flour
100 g butter
salt
freshly ground black pepper
25 g flaked almonds

To garnish:
1 lemon, quartered
2 × 15 ml spoons chopped
   fresh parsley

Imperial
4 × 6 oz trout, cleaned
4 tablespoons milk
2 oz flour
4 oz butter
salt
freshly ground black pepper
1 oz flaked almonds

To garnish:
1 lemon, quartered
2 tablespoons chopped
   fresh parsley

Cooking time: 15 minutes

Rinse and dry the fish. Dip in milk, then coat in flour, shaking off the excess. Melt 75 g/3 oz of the butter in a heavy frying pan and fry the fish over a brisk heat until golden brown, turning once, with care. Arrange the fish on a hot serving dish and season with salt and pepper. Keep warm. Wipe out the pan, melt the remaining butter and fry the almonds, turning constantly, until they are also golden. Pour over the fish and garnish with lemon and parsley.

Devilled sardines

Metric
500 g sardines
1 × 15 ml spoon made
   mustard
1 × 15 ml spoon
   Worcestershire sauce
pinch of paprika
small bunch of watercress,
   to garnish
Niçoise Sauce (page 71),
   to serve

Imperial
1 lb sardines
1 tablespoon made
   mustard
1 tablespoon
   Worcestershire sauce
pinch of paprika
small bunch of watercress,
   to garnish
Niçoise sauce (page 71),
   to serve

Cooking time: 6 minutes

There is no need to gut fresh sardines.

Rinse the fish quickly and dry them, then lay them on a greased baking sheet. Mix the mustard with the Worcestershire sauce and brush the fish with it. Cook under a hot grill for 3 minutes. Turn the fish over carefully and brush again with the mustard mixture. Grill for another 3 minutes to finish cooking. Sprinkle the fish with paprika, then serve very hot, garnished with watercress and accompanied with fingers of toast and niçoise sauce.

Devilled sardines

Trout with almonds; Trout en gelée vert

Trout en gelée vert

Metric	Imperial
150 ml dry white wine	*¼ pint dry white wine*
300 ml water	*½ pint water*
1 × 15 ml spoon white	*1 tablespoon white wine*
* wine vinegar*	* vinegar*
1 carrot, scraped and sliced	*1 carrot, scraped and sliced*
1 onion, peeled and	*1 onion, peeled and*
* stuck with a clove*	* stuck with a clove*
1 bay leaf	*1 bay leaf*
2 sprigs of marjoram	*2 sprigs of marjoram*
sprig of thyme	*sprig of thyme*
2 sprigs of parsley	*2 sprigs of parsley*
12 peppercorns	*12 peppercorns*
1 × 2.5 ml spoon salt	*½ teaspoon salt*
2 strips of orange rind	*2 strips of orange rind*
4 × 175 g trout,	*4 × 6 oz trout,*
* cleaned and trimmed*	* cleaned and trimmed*
3 × 15 ml spoons finely	*3 tablespoons finely*
* chopped fresh parsley*	* chopped fresh parsley*

To garnish:
4 unpeeled orange slices
1 lettuce heart,
* quartered*

To garnish:
4 unpeeled orange slices
1 lettuce heart,
* quartered*

Cooking time: 30 minutes

Put all the ingredients, except the fish and chopped parsley, into a large pan. Cover and bring slowly to the boil, then simmer for 20 minutes. Allow to cool, then strain.

Lay the fish in a large sauté or frying pan and pour over the cold liquid. Bring carefully to the boil and immediately reduce the heat. Simmer the fish for 7 to 8 minutes. Lift them on to a board, skin and remove the fillets. Arrange the fish on a serving dish. Add the bones, heads, skin, etc. to the liquid in the pan and reduce by boiling rapidly until there is just enough liquid to cover the fish. Allow to cool, then chill for at least 1 hour. Add the chopped parsley and pour over the trout. Garnish with twists of orange and lettuce. Serve mayonnaise separately.

SHELLFISH

The flesh of lobster and crab is dense and long fibred, tending to make it rather difficult to digest. The meat is found largely in the tail and claws, the body consisting mainly of the liver. The use of lemon juice or vinegar helps to soften the fibres. As in the case of white fish the methods and recipes for both crustacea and molluscs are interchangeable, particularly where similar types are used.

Shellfish is versatile and can be served in many different ways. Because there is a high percentage of waste, due to shell, it is expensive and looked upon as an occasional treat. When there is only a small amount available, combine it with a sauce of your choice and use as a filling for vol-au-vents or crêpes or as a stuffing for simple fish such as boned whiting. Alternatively, shellfish can be made into fritters and deep-fried or alternated with other ingredients on skewers then grilled and served with a sharp spicy sauce. Shellfish deteriorates rapidly, so absolute freshness is essential.

Mussels Italian style

Cooking time: about 25 minutes
Oven: 180°C, 350°F, Gas Mark 4

Metric	Imperial
1¾ kg mussels, washed, scrubbed and bearded	4 lb mussels, washed, scrubbed and bearded
bouquet garni	bouquet garni
120 ml water	4 fl oz water
120 ml dry white wine	4 fl oz dry white wine
pinch of salt	pinch of salt
freshly ground black pepper	freshly ground black pepper
2 × 15 ml spoons finely chopped shallot	2 tablespoons finely chopped shallot
1 garlic clove, peeled and crushed	1 garlic clove, peeled and crushed
2 × 15 ml spoons finely chopped fresh parsley	2 tablespoons finely chopped fresh parsley
75 g fresh brown breadcrumbs	3 oz fresh brown breadcrumbs
3 × 15 ml spoons grated Parmesan cheese	3 tablespoons grated Parmesan cheese
25 g butter	1 oz butter

Place the mussels in a deep pan, add the bouquet garni and pour over the water and wine, then add salt and pepper. Cover the pan and cook over a brisk heat until the mussels open, about 5 minutes. Shake the pan occasionally. Strain and reserve the liquor. Remove the empty half of each shell, then place the remaining shells, mussel side up, close together in a large shallow ovenproof dish. Sprinkle them with the shallot, garlic, parsley, breadcrumbs and finally the cheese. Dot the butter over the dish.

In a small pan, reduce the fish liquor to half by boiling rapidly, then pour round, not over, the dish. Bake in a preheated moderate oven for 15 to 20 minutes. Serve very hot with crusty French bread.

Prawn and cream cheese pâté

Metric	Imperial
175 g cream cheese	6 oz cream cheese
3 spring onions or 1 shallot, peeled and very finely chopped	3 spring onions or 1 shallot, peeled and very finely chopped
250 g peeled prawns or shrimps	9 oz peeled prawns or shrimps
juice of 1 small lemon	juice of 1 small lemon
salt	salt
freshly ground black pepper	freshly ground black pepper
1½ × 15 ml spoons finely chopped fresh dill or fennel	1½ tablespoons finely chopped fresh dill or fennel

To garnish:
halved black olives
fronds of dill or fennel

To garnish:
halved black olives
fronds of dill or fennel

In a mixing bowl, beat the cream cheese with a wooden spoon until it is smooth. Add the onion or shallot. Chop the prawns and stir into the cheese mixture. Add the lemon juice, season well with salt and pepper, then add the herb. Mix well together, then divide the mixture between 4 cocottes or small individual dishes. Smooth the tops. Garnish with olives and dill or fennel fronds.

Mussels Italian style; Prawn and cream cheese pâté

Seafood risotto

Metric	Imperial
4 × 15 ml spoons oil	4 tablespoons oil
275 g Italian rice	10 oz Italian rice
2 medium onions, peeled and finely sliced	2 medium onions, peeled and finely sliced
salt	salt
freshly ground black pepper	freshly ground black pepper
900 ml hot chicken stock	1½ pints hot chicken stock
75 g butter	3 oz butter
350 g cooked, cold seafood	12 oz cooked, cold seafood
1 × 2.5 ml spoon grated nutmeg	½ teaspoon grated nutmeg
1 × 5 ml spoon turmeric	1 teaspoon turmeric
1 × 5 ml spoon golden syrup	1 teaspoon golden syrup
juice of ½ lemon	juice of ½ lemon
2 × 15 ml spoons double cream	2 tablespoons double cream

To garnish:
unpeeled prawns
fronds of dill or fennel
50 g grated Parmesan cheese, to serve

To garnish:
unpeeled prawns
fronds of dill or fennel
2 oz grated Parmesan cheese, to serve

Cooking time: about 40 minutes

A mixture of any shellfish may be used, such as lobster, crab, prawn, shrimp, mussels or cockles. Use Italian rice to give a good flavour, it is available from most delicatessens.

Heat the oil in a large frying pan, then add the rice, onion and a little salt and pepper to taste. Cook gently for 5 minutes, stirring constantly. Add 300 ml/½ pint of the stock and continue to simmer until the liquid is almost absorbed, about 10 minutes, then add another 300 ml/½ pint of the stock. Continue in this way until the rice is cooked (soft but not mushy). Do not allow it to dry up, a risotto is moist. When cooked, lightly fork in 25 g/1 oz of the butter. Cover and keep warm. Melt the butter in a pan and add the chosen seafood, stir in the nutmeg, turmeric, syrup and lemon juice, heat through gently and stir in the cream. Turn the hot rice into a large warmed serving dish. Top with the seafood mixture and garnish with prawns and dill or fennel. Serve the cheese separately.

Seafood risotto

Cockles in cream; Fried scallops with bacon

Cockles in cream

Metric
1½ *kg cockles*
25 g butter
few parsley stalks
1 onion, peeled and sliced
150 ml dry white wine
150 ml double cream
salt
freshly ground black pepper
1 × 15 ml spoon chopped
fresh parsley, to garnish

Imperial
3 lb cockles
1 oz butter
few parsley stalks
1 onion, peeled and sliced
¼ pint dry white wine
¼ pint double cream
salt
freshly ground black pepper
1 tablespoon chopped
fresh parsley, to garnish

Cooking time: about 10 minutes

Steep the cockles for an hour or two in fresh water, then wash them well in more fresh cold water. Put them in a pan with the butter and parsley stalks and onion, then add the wine. Cover and cook for 4 minutes over a brisk heat. Strain the liquor into a small pan, and reserve. Remove the cockles from the shells with a pin, then keep them warm. Reduce the liquor to half by boiling rapidly. Remove from the heat, stir in the cream and season to taste with salt and pepper. Reheat carefully, but do not allow to boil. Put the cockles into a hot serving dish, pour over the sauce and sprinkle with the dill or fennel.

Fried scallops with bacon

Metric
8 large scallops
50 g flour
salt
freshly ground black pepper
2 eggs, beaten
75 g soft white
breadcrumbs
oil for deep frying
8 streaky bacon rashers,
de-rinded

Imperial
8 large scallops
2 oz flour
salt
freshly ground black pepper
2 eggs, beaten
3 oz soft white
breadcrumbs
oil for deep frying
8 streaky bacon rashers,
de-rinded

Cooking time: 10 to 15 minutes

Open and clean the scallops, then rinse and dry them well. Season the flour with salt and pepper. Dip the scallops into flour, egg and then breadcrumbs, pressing them on. Heat the oil to 190°C/375°F and carefully lower the scallops into it. Cook until lightly coloured, no more than 5 minutes. Remove and drain on kitchen paper. Keep hot.
Cut the bacon slices in half, then roll up, securing with wooden cocktail sticks. Grill or fry the bacon until crisp and drain on kitchen paper. Arrange the scallops on a hot serving dish with the bacon rolls. Serve with a tartare sauce.

Seafood crêpes

Metric	Imperial
100 g plain flour	4 oz plain flour
salt	salt
2 eggs	2 eggs
300 ml milk	½ pint milk
1 × 15 ml spoon oil	1 tablespoon oil
oil for cooking	oil for cooking

Filling:	Filling:
300 ml Bechamel Sauce (page 68)	½ pint Bechamel Sauce (page 68)
175 g prepared crab meat	6 oz prepared crab meat
175 g peeled prawns	6 oz peeled prawns
2 × 5 ml spoons chopped fresh dill or fennel	2 teaspoons chopped fresh dill or fennel
freshly ground black pepper	freshly ground black pepper
2 tomatoes, skinned and sliced	2 tomatoes, skinned and sliced
50 g Cheddar cheese, grated	2 oz Cheddar cheese, grated
sprigs of watercress, to garnish	sprigs of watercress, to garnish

Cooking time: 30 minutes

Sift the flour with a pinch of salt into a bowl. Make a well in the centre, drop in the eggs and stir in half the milk. Stir together with a wooden spoon until smooth, then beat well with a whisk. Add the remaining milk, mix well and leave for at least 30 minutes.
When ready to make the crêpes, stir in the oil. Make the pancakes and keep them warm in a folded clean tea towel.
Bring the sauce to the boil, remove from the heat and add the crab meat, prawns, herb, and salt and pepper to taste. Divide the mixture between the pancakes and roll them up. Place them in a lightly greased oven-proof dish and lay the tomato slices over them. Sprinkle with the cheese and grill until golden and bubbling. Garnish with watercress and serve immediately.
Makes about 8

From left: Seafood crêpes; Prawn fritters; Prawn and mushroom vol-au-vent

Prawn fritters

Metric	Imperial
100 g flour	4 oz flour
2 eggs	2 eggs
200 ml milk	⅓ pint milk
salt	salt
freshly ground black pepper	freshly ground black pepper
225 g peeled prawns, chopped	8 oz peeled prawns, chopped
cooking oil	cooking oil
fronds of dill or fennel, to garnish	fronds of dill or fennel, to garnish

Cooking time: about 6 minutes

Sift the flour into a bowl, then make a well in the centre. Drop in the eggs and add a little of the milk. Beat well with a wooden spoon until smooth. Stir in the remaining milk and season well with salt and pepper. Set aside for 30 minutes, then fold in the prawns.
Heat 1 cm/½ inch of oil in a frying pan. Drop dessertspoonfuls of the mixture into the oil and fry until crisp and golden on both sides. Drain on kitchen paper. Arrange the fritters overlapping on a heated serving dish. Garnish with dill or fennel. Serve with a bearnaise sauce.

Prawn and mushroom vol-au-vent

Cooking time: 35 to 40 minutes
Oven: 220°C, 425°F, Gas Mark 7

Metric	Imperial
375 g frozen puff pastry, defrosted	13 oz frozen puff pastry, defrosted
1 small egg, beaten	1 small egg, beaten

Filling:
25 g butter
100 g button mushrooms, quartered
150 ml Fish Velouté Sauce (page 72)
squeeze of lemon juice
salt
pinch of cayenne
175 g peeled prawns
sprig of parsley, to garnish

Filling:
1 oz butter
4 oz button mushrooms, quartered
¼ pint Fish Velouté Sauce (page 72)
squeeze of lemon juice
salt
pinch of cayenne
6 oz peeled prawns
sprig of parsley, to garnish

To make the vol-au-vent, roll out the pastry on a floured board to 1 cm/½ inch thickness. Place a 15 cm/6 inch pan lid on the pastry and cut around it with a knife, holding it at an angle, to get a disc wider at the base. Run cold water over a baking sheet and invert the pastry on to it. Brush the top with beaten egg.

Take a 10 cm/4 inch pan lid or cutter and, using a knife, mark a circle round the lid, in the centre of the pastry. Lightly mark the centre and edges with a lattice design if liked, then chill the pastry for 10 minutes.

Bake in the centre of a preheated hot oven for 30 minutes. Remove from the oven, and allow to cool a little. Carefully cut around the pastry lid, lift it off and set aside. Using a spoon, remove some of the soft pastry from the inside of the pastry shell.

Melt the butter in a pan and fry the mushrooms for 3 minutes. Add the velouté sauce, lemon juice and salt and cayenne to taste. Bring to the boil, remove from the heat and stir in the prawns. Reheat carefully, without boiling. Meanwhile put the vol-au-vent case back into the oven for 5 minutes. Place it on a hot serving dish, fill with the prawn mixture, replace the pastry lid at an angle and garnish with parsley.

Crab cobbler

Crab cobbler

Cooking time: 35 minutes
Oven: 220°C, 425°F, Gas Mark 7

Metric
75 g butter
1 green pepper, cored,
    seeded and diced
1 medium onion, peeled
    and finely sliced
50 g flour
1 × 5 ml spoon dry mustard
250 ml milk
75 g Cheddar cheese, grated
225 g prepared crab meat
350 g ripe tomatoes,
    skinned and diced
2 × 5 ml spoons
    Worcestershire sauce
salt
freshly ground black pepper

Cheese scone topping:
100 g plain flour
salt
freshly ground black pepper
2 × 5 ml spoons baking
    powder
50 g butter or shortening
25 g Cheddar cheese, grated
milk to mix

Imperial
3 oz butter
1 green pepper, cored,
    seeded and diced
1 medium onion, peeled
    and finely sliced
2 oz flour
1 teaspoon dry mustard
8 fl oz milk
3 oz Cheddar cheese, grated
8 oz prepared crab meat
12 oz ripe tomatoes,
    skinned and diced
2 teaspoons
    Worcestershire sauce
salt
freshly ground black pepper

Cheese scone topping:
4 oz plain flour
salt
freshly ground black pepper
2 teaspoons baking
    powder
2 oz butter or shortening
1 oz Cheddar cheese, grated
milk to mix

The top of this dish should resemble cobblestones, therefore the topping dough must be stiff, otherwise it flattens in cooking and the effect is lost.

Melt the butter in a saucepan over a gentle heat and cook the green pepper and onion together until tender, about 10 minutes. Remove from the heat and blend in the flour, then the mustard and milk. Return to the heat and cook, stirring constantly, until the mixture is very thick. Add the cheese and reheat until melted. Stir in the crab, tomatoes, Worcestershire sauce and salt and pepper to taste. Turn the mixture into an ovenproof dish.

To make the topping, sift the flour, salt, pepper and baking powder into a bowl. Rub in the fat until the mixture resembles fine breadcrumbs. Stir in the cheese with a knife and mix to a stiff dough with a little milk. Mould the dough into small balls and place on top of the crab meat mixture and bake in a preheated hot oven for 15 to 20 minutes. Serve with a green salad.

Shrimp jambalaya

Metric	Imperial
4 rashers of bacon, de-rinded and diced	4 rashers of bacon, de-rinded and diced
1 small onion, peeled and finely sliced	1 small onion, peeled and finely sliced
1 garlic clove, crushed	1 garlic clove, crushed
½ green pepper, cored, seeded and diced	½ green pepper, cored, seeded and diced
75 g rice	3 oz rice
350 ml chicken stock	12 fl oz chicken stock
225 g ripe tomatoes, skinned, seeded and diced	8 oz ripe tomatoes, skinned, seeded and diced
1 bay leaf	1 bay leaf
1 × 2.5 ml spoon chilli powder	½ teaspoon chilli powder
1 × 2.5 ml spoon chopped fresh basil	½ teaspoon chopped fresh basil
salt	salt
freshly ground black pepper	freshly ground black pepper
225 g peeled shrimps	8 oz peeled shrimps
50 g green or black olives, pitted and sliced (optional)	2 oz green or black olives, pitted and sliced (optional)

Cooking time: 35 to 40 minutes

Fry the bacon until crisp, drain and put on a plate. Add the onion, garlic and green pepper to the pan and cook gently until soft. Replace the bacon and add the remaining ingredients, except the shrimps and olives. Bring to the boil, cover and simmer for 15 to 20 minutes or until the rice is tender. Add the shrimps and olives (if using), then heat through until hot. Remove the bay leaf and turn into a hot serving dish.

Prawn gratin

Metric	Imperial
225 g peeled prawns	8 oz peeled prawns
2 hard-boiled eggs, chopped	2 hard-boiled eggs, chopped
4 tomatoes, skinned and sliced	4 tomatoes, skinned and sliced
1 × 5 ml spoon paprika	1 teaspoon paprika
300 ml Cheese Sauce (page 69)	½ pint Cheese Sauce (page 69)
1 × 15 ml spoon cream (optional)	1 tablespoon cream (optional)
salt	salt
freshly ground black pepper	freshly ground black pepper
25 g Gruyère or Emmental cheese, grated	1 oz Gruyère or Emmental cheese, grated

Cooking time: 15 minutes
Oven: 190°C, 375°F, Gas Mark 5

This makes a good first course if there is something light to follow.

Butter an ovenproof dish and arrange in it the prawns, eggs and tomatoes, in layers. Stir the paprika into the sauce and bring to the boil. Add the cream, if using, and salt and pepper to taste, then pour over the dish. Sprinkle with the cheese and bake in a preheated moderately hot oven for 15 minutes.

Shrimp jambalaya; Prawn gratin

Prawn doria

Metric	Imperial
1 large cucumber, peeled and finely grated	1 large cucumber, peeled and finely grated
about 300 ml water	about ½ pint water
white wine vinegar to taste	white wine vinegar to taste
lemon juice to taste	lemon juice to taste
salt	salt
freshly ground pepper	freshly ground pepper
15 g (1 envelope) powdered gelatine or aspic	½ oz (1 envelope) powdered gelatine or aspic
2 × 15 ml spoons cold water	2 tablespoons cold water
350 g peeled prawns	12 oz peeled prawns
300 ml Tomato Mayonnaise (page 76)	½ pint Tomato Mayonnaise (page 76)

To garnish:
twists of unpeeled
  cucumber
few unpeeled prawns

To garnish:
twists of unpeeled
  cucumber
few unpeeled prawns

Put the cucumber into a measuring jug and make up to 600 ml/1 pint with the water. Add wine vinegar, lemon juice and salt and pepper to taste. Soak the gelatine or aspic in the water, then dissolve over a low heat. Allow to cool slightly, then stir into the mixture. Turn at once into an oiled 900 ml/1½ pint ring mould and leave in a cool place to set, about 20 minutes. Mix the prawns with 150 ml/¼ pint of the tomato mayonnaise. When the cucumber mould is set, turn it out carefully on to a serving dish. Fill the centre with the prawns and garnish with cucumber twists and unpeeled prawns. Serve the remaining mayonnaise separately.

Crab and bacon olives

Metric	Imperial
175 g prepared crab meat	6 oz prepared crab meat
1 small egg, beaten	1 small egg, beaten
75 g soft breadcrumbs	3 oz soft breadcrumbs
120 ml tomato juice	4 fl oz tomato juice
1 × 5 ml spoon chopped basil	1 teaspoon chopped basil
1 × 5 ml spoon chopped parsley	1 teaspoon chopped parsley
salt	salt
freshly ground black pepper	freshly ground black pepper
12 back bacon rashers, de-rinded	12 back bacon rashers, de-rinded

To garnish:
tomato wedges
sprigs of watercress

To garnish:
tomato wedges
sprigs of watercress

Mix together the crab meat, egg, breadcrumbs and enough of the tomato juice to bind. Add the basil, parsley and salt and pepper to taste. Mix well together and shape into 12 fingers. Wrap a bacon rasher round each one, then secure with a wooden cocktail stick. Place on a rack under a preheated grill and cook until the bacon is crisp, turning frequently. Arrange on a hot dish and garnish with the tomatoes and watercress.

Crab and bacon olives

Dressed crab

Metric
2 × 750 g crabs
salt
freshly ground black pepper
1.2 litres Court Bouillon
  (page 60), or salted
  water with 1 × 15 ml
  spoon vinegar
a little oil
3 × 15 ml spoons fresh
  white breadcrumbs
1 × 5 ml spoon prepared
  mustard
salt
freshly ground black pepper

To garnish:
2 hard-boiled eggs,
  yolks sieved, whites
  finely chopped
cayenne

Imperial
2 × 1½ lb crabs
salt
freshly ground black pepper
2 pints Court Bouillon
  (page 60), or salted
  water with 1
  tablespoon vinegar
a little oil
3 tablespoons fresh
  white breadcrumbs
1 teaspoon prepared
  mustard
salt
freshly ground black pepper

To garnish:
2 hard-boiled eggs,
  yolks sieved, whites
  finely chopped
cayenne

Cooking time: 15 to 20 minutes

Wash and cook the crabs, allowing 10 minutes to the 500 g/1 lb from boiling point. Cool.

To dress the crabs, twist off the large claws. Lift the flap underneath the crab and remove the body and small claws. Discard the sac lying at the top of the big shell, also any green matter and the grey spongy lungs, which are known as 'dead man's fingers'.

Scrape all the brown creamy meat into a small bowl. Tap around the natural line on the underside and press off and discard the surplus shell. Wash the remaining shell well and dry it. Rub with a little oil.

Cut the body of the crab in half and, with a skewer, pick out the white meat. Put the meat in a separate bowl, taking care not to include any small fragments of shell. Crack the large claws and add the meat to the bowl, breaking it up well.

Cream the brown meat with a wooden spoon, add the breadcrumbs, mustard and salt and pepper to taste. Taste and add more mustard if liked. Turn this mixture into the centre of the shell and pile the white meat neatly either side. Garnish with the egg and sprinkle with cayenne. Serve with mayonnaise or French dressing and brown bread and butter.

Dressed crab; Prawn Doria

Moules marinière

Metric
1¾ kg mussels
3 shallots or 1 small onion,
    peeled and finely
    chopped
1 garlic clove, peeled and
    crushed
sprig of parsley
sprig of thyme
1 bay leaf
40 g butter
250 ml dry white wine
salt
freshly ground black pepper
1 × 15 ml spoon finely
    chopped fresh parsley,
    to garnish

Imperial
4 lb mussels
3 shallots or 1 small onion,
    peeled and finely
    chopped
1 garlic clove, peeled and
    crushed
sprig of parsley
sprig of thyme
1 bay leaf
1½ oz butter
8 fl oz dry white wine
salt
freshly ground black pepper
1 tablespoon finely
    chopped fresh parsley,
    to garnish

Cooking time: 7 to 8 minutes

Fresh mussels have tightly closed shells. Discard any that are cracked or open even if only slightly so. If it is necessary to keep them overnight, wash and scrub them well, then put in a bucket full of sea or salted water. Sprinkle with oatmeal, cover the bucket with a tea towel and leave in a cool place.

Wash and scrub the mussels well, discarding any open or cracked ones. With a small, sharp, strong knife, scrape away the beard and anything else attached to the shell. When they have all been scraped, wash them again in several waters until there is no sand at the bottom of the bowl.

Put the mussels into a large pan with the rest of the ingredients, adding salt and pepper. Cover the pan and shake over a brisk heat for about 5 minutes until all the shells have opened. Divide the mussels between 4 hot soup plates or bowls and keep hot while you reduce the liquor by boiling for 3 minutes. Strain over the mussels and sprinkle with parsley. Serve with plenty of crusty French bread.

Variations:
For a thicker sauce, stir in 3 × 15 ml spoons/3 table-spoons double cream or 25 g/1 oz beurre manié after reducing the liquor, then reheat until thickened.

From front: Crab salad Waldorf; Swedish shellfish cocktail

Moules marinière

Crab salad Waldorf

Metric	Imperial
1 × 750 g crab, cooked and cooled	1 × 1½ lb crab, cooked and cooled
2 crisp dessert apples, peeled, cored and diced	2 crisp dessert apples, peeled, cored and diced
1 celery stick, finely sliced	1 celery stick, finely sliced
25 g walnut pieces, coarsely chopped	1 oz walnut pieces, coarsely chopped
1 garlic clove, peeled and crushed	1 garlic clove, peeled and crushed
4 × 15 ml spoons mayonnaise	4 tablespoons mayonnaise
1 × 15 ml spoon snipped chives	1 tablespoon snipped chives
squeeze lemon juice	squeeze lemon juice
salt	salt
freshly ground black pepper	freshly ground black pepper
pinch dry mustard	pinch dry mustard
few drops wine vinegar	few drops wine vinegar
1 lettuce heart, rinsed and dried	1 lettuce heart, rinsed and dried

To garnish:
twists of lemon
black Danish caviare
(optional)

Remove the crab meat, putting the white and brown meat in separate bowls. Combine the white crab meat, apple, celery, walnuts and garlic. Stir in the mayonnaise, chives, lemon juice and season well with salt and pepper. Add the mustard to the brown crab meat and season to taste with salt, pepper and vinegar.
Line 4 scallop shells or shallow individual dishes with the lettuce. Divide the white meat mixture equally between them, and top with the brown meat. Garnish with lemon twists and caviare, if liked.

Swedish shellfish cocktail

Metric	Imperial
4 outer leaves lettuce, washed and dried	4 outer leaves lettuce, washed and dried
225 g shellfish, composed of white crab meat, lobster and shrimps or prawns	8 oz shellfish, composed of white crab meat, lobster and shrimps or prawns
50 g button mushrooms, finely sliced	2 oz button mushrooms, finely sliced
100 g cooked cold green peas	4 oz cooked cold green peas
150 ml Rémoulade Sauce (page 74)	¼ pint Rémoulade Sauce (page 74)
salt	salt
freshly ground black pepper	freshly ground black pepper

To garnish:
sprigs of parsley
4 whole cooked prawns

Make a chiffonade. To do this, place the lettuce leaves one on top of the other, then roll up tightly like a cigar. With a very sharp knife, shred it finely. Toss up the shreds with a fork. Half fill 4 individual wine goblets with the shredded lettuce.
Mix together the flaked crab meat, lobster and the shrimps or prawns. Stir in the mushrooms and peas and mix all together with the rémoulade sauce. Add salt and pepper to taste. Spoon the mixture on top of the lettuce in the glasses and garnish with parsley and prawns.

PRESERVED FISH

Before easy transport and refrigeration came into being the harvest of the rivers and seas had to be preserved. There were several ways of doing this and some of those methods are still used. The freshly caught fish was often lightly or heavily salted and threaded on washing lines to dry; this was customary in parts of Scotland until very recently.

In certain fish a combination of salting and smoking (either cool or hot) is applied. Apart from giving a very distinctive flavour, the creosote, alcohols, tar, formaldehyde and acids present in wood smoke have a bactericidal effect. The herring is subjected to several different treatments to turn it into either a salt herring, bloater, kipper or buckling. Kippers, bloaters, haddocks, golden cutlets (whiting), cod and salmon are cool smoked at 32°C/90°F. Eel, buckling, trout, sprats, Arbroath smokies and mackerel are hot smoked at 100°C/212°F. Generally speaking cool smoked fish needs cooking and hot smoked does not. The obvious exception to this is smoked salmon, but kipper fillets can be marinated and eaten uncooked.

Kipper cutlets

Metric
4 kippers or 2 × 225 g
* packets of fillets,*
* poached and flaked*
175 g potato purée
25 g butter
2 × 5 ml spoons chopped
* fresh parsley*
1 × 5 ml spoon lemon juice
salt
freshly ground black pepper
1 egg, beaten
a little milk
100 g fresh white
* breadcrumbs*
oil for deep frying
deep-fried parsley
* sprigs, to garnish*

Imperial
4 kippers or 2 × 8 oz
* packets of fillets,*
* poached and flaked*
6 oz potato purée
1 oz butter
2 teaspoons chopped
* fresh parsley*
1 teaspoon lemon juice
salt
freshly ground black pepper
1 egg, beaten
a little milk
4 oz fresh white
* breadcrumbs*
oil for deep frying
deep-fried parsley
* sprigs, to garnish*

Cooking time: about 8 minutes

Prepared instant potato may be used for this. If liked, the kipper may be shaped into round flat cakes or fish shapes instead of cutlets.

In a pan mix together the fish, potato, butter, parsley, lemon juice and salt and pepper to taste. Stir in enough of the egg to bind the mixture lightly. Heat the mixture, beating with a wooden spoon, until well blended. Allow it to cool a little, then turn on to a floured surface. Divide into 8 equal sized pieces and shape each piece into cutlets. Add a little milk to the remaining egg and dip the cutlets into the egg mixture, then coat in breadcrumbs. Heat the oil to 190°C/375°F, lower 4 cutlets into it and fry for about 4 minutes. Drain on kitchen paper, keep hot, and fry the remaining cutlets. Arrange the cutlets on a hot serving dish and garnish with fried parsley.

Scrambled kippers

Metric
50 g butter
2 spring onions or 1
* shallot, peeled and*
* chopped*
4 eggs
2 × 15 ml spoons top
* of the milk*
2 kippers, or 1 × 225 g
* packet of fillets,*
* poached and flaked*
1 × 15 ml spoon chopped
* fresh parsley*
salt
freshly ground black pepper

To garnish:
crisp crescents of fried
* bread*

Imperial
2 oz butter
2 spring onions or 1
* shallot, peeled and*
* chopped*
4 eggs
2 tablespoons top of
* the milk*
2 kippers, or 1 × 8 oz
* packet of fillets,*
* poached and flaked*
1 tablespoon chopped
* fresh parsley*
salt
freshly ground black pepper

To garnish:
crisp crescents of fried
* bread*

Cooking time: 8 to 10 minutes

This makes a delicious breakfast or supper dish.

Melt the butter in a saucepan, add the onion and soften over a low heat. Beat the eggs lightly, just enough to break them up, then add the top of the milk, kipper flesh, parsley and salt and pepper to taste. Pour the mixture into the butter and onion and cook slowly until soft and creamy, stirring with a wooden spoon. Serve on a hot dish garnished with crescents of fried bread.

Kipper cutlets; Scrambled kippers

Buckling pâté

Metric
1 large buckling,
  skinned and boned
150 g unsalted butter,
  softened
1 × 15 ml spoon lemon
  juice
1 garlic clove, peeled
  and crushed
good pinch of ground
  mace or nutmeg
freshly ground black pepper
small fresh bay leaves,
  to garnish

Imperial
1 large buckling,
  skinned and boned
5 oz unsalted butter,
  softened
1 tablespoon lemon
  juice
1 garlic clove, peeled
  and crushed
good pinch of ground
  mace or nutmeg
freshly ground black pepper
small fresh bay leaves,
  to garnish

The distinctive flavour of buckling lends itself to pâté. This freezes well and is useful as a standby first course or for using on canapés, in sandwiches or stuffing hard-boiled eggs, etc.

Pound the buckling flesh with the butter, adding the lemon juice a little at a time, the garlic, mace or nutmeg and black pepper. Work it all together until well blended. Put the mixture into 4 individual pots, garnishing each with a bay leaf. Serve slightly chilled with very hot crisp toast.

Smoked haddock mayonnaise

Metric
500 g smoked haddock
  fillet
1 bay leaf
slice of onion
freshly ground black pepper
bunch of watercress
225 g green peas, cooked
300 ml Herb Mayonnaise
  (page 75)
pinch of paprika

Imperial
1 lb smoked haddock
  fillet
1 bay leaf
slice of onion
freshly ground black pepper
bunch of watercress
8 oz green peas, cooked
½ pint Herb Mayonnaise
  (page 75)
pinch of paprika

Cooking time: about 15 minutes

Serve as a first course, or a main course accompanied by a salad.

Place the fish in a pan and cover with cold water, then add the bay leaf and onion and a little pepper. Bring to the boil, cover and poach for 10 to 15 minutes. Drain the fish, then remove the skin.
Divide the fish into 4 equal portions and leave until cold. Lay the watercress on a chilled serving dish and arrange the fish and peas on it. Coat each serving with the well seasoned mayonnaise and finish with a sprinkling of paprika.

Winesap baskets

Metric	Imperial
4 red skinned eating apples	4 red skinned eating apples
juice of 1 large lemon	juice of 1 large lemon
1 × 175 g smoked buckling, skinned and filleted	1 × 6 oz smoked buckling, skinned and filleted
50 g grapes, pips removed	2 oz grapes, pips removed
8 black olives	8 black olives
50 g salted peanuts	2 oz salted peanuts
2–3 × 15 ml spoons mayonnaise	2–3 tablespoons mayonnaise
50 g cream cheese	2 oz cream cheese
salt	salt
freshly ground black pepper	freshly ground black pepper
2 × 15 ml spoons finely chopped chives or spring onions	2 tablespoons finely chopped chives or spring onions
bunch of watercress	bunch of watercress
sprigs of mint, to garnish	sprigs of mint, to garnish

Cut a slice off the top of each apple and carefully remove the core and flesh, using a grapefruit knife or teaspoon, leaving a thin wall. Brush the inside with a little of the lemon juice to prevent discolouration. Dice the apple flesh and soak it in lemon juice.

Cut the fish into bite-sized pieces. Combine with the grapes, olives, salted peanuts and the drained apple flesh, then stir in enough mayonnaise to bind. Season the cream cheese and form into small balls, roll in the chives or onion and place on the apples. Arrange the watercress on the bottom of a serving dish and place the apples on top. Garnish each apple with a mint sprig. Serve chilled with a bowl of mayonnaise.

Variations:
Substitute smoked trout, cold cooked kipper or bloater for the smoked buckling.

From left: Buckling pâté; Winesap baskets; Smoked haddock mayonnaise

Kedgeree

Metric
500 g smoked haddock fillet
75 g butter
1 onion, peeled and
  finely sliced
1 × 2.5 ml spoon curry
  powder
100 g long grain rice
squeeze of lemon juice
50 g sultanas
600 ml chicken stock
4 × 15 ml spoons
  chopped fresh parsley
salt
freshly ground black pepper

To garnish:
2 hard-boiled eggs, sliced
1 lemon, quartered

Imperial
1 lb smoked haddock fillet
3 oz butter
1 onion, peeled and
  finely sliced
½ teaspoon curry
  powder
4 oz long grain rice
squeeze of lemon juice
2 oz sultanas
1 pint chicken stock
4 tablespoons chopped
  fresh parsley
salt
freshly ground black pepper

To garnish:
2 hard-boiled eggs, sliced
1 lemon, quartered

Kedgeree

Cooking time: about 25 minutes

To make a good kedgeree you must be generous with the butter. Do not wash the rice, which removes some of the starch so necessary for the creamy consistency.

Place the fillet in a shallow dish and cover with boiling water. Leave for 3 minutes. Drain the fish, then remove and discard the skin and any bones. Flake the flesh. Melt 25 g/1 oz of the butter in a large frying pan, add the onion and cook gently until soft. Add the curry powder and cook for 2 minutes, then stir in the rice, lemon juice and sultanas and pour on the stock. Bring to the boil and cook steadily for 15 minutes. Add the fish and continue cooking very gently for about 10 minutes, or until the rice is tender and the liquid absorbed.

Using a fork, stir in the remaining butter and the parsley, then add salt and pepper to taste. Transfer to a hot serving dish and garnish with the eggs and lemon. Serve with sweet chutney and fried bread fingers, if liked.

From left: Jansson's temptation; Smoked mackerel tart

Jansson's temptation

Metric
12 anchovy fillets or
  1 × 50 g can
500 g potatoes, peeled
  and cut into match-
  sticks
2 large onions, peeled
  and finely sliced
1 garlic clove, peeled
  and crushed
1 × 15 ml spoon chopped
  fresh parsley
freshly ground black pepper
300 ml single cream
40 g butter

Imperial
12 anchovy fillets or
  1 × 2 oz can
1 lb potatoes, peeled
  and cut into match-
  sticks
2 large onions, peeled
  and finely sliced
1 garlic clove, peeled
  and crushed
1 tablespoon chopped
  fresh parsley
freshly ground black pepper
$\frac{1}{2}$ pint single cream
$1\frac{1}{2}$ oz butter

Cooking time: about 1 hour
Oven: 220°C, 425°F, Gas Mark 7

If using canned anchovies, drain and reserve a little of the liquid. Cut each fillet into 4 pieces. Well butter an ovenproof dish then layer in it the potatoes, onions, garlic, anchovies and parsley, seasoning with black pepper and finishing with a layer of potatoes. Drizzle on a little of the anchovy liquid, if available. Pour over half the cream and dot the butter over the top. Bake in a preheated hot oven until the potatoes are lightly coloured, then pour over the remaining cream and continue cooking until the potatoes are tender. Serve with a green salad.

Smoked mackerel tart

Metric
225 g flour
pinch of salt
100 g butter
1 egg, beaten

For the filling:
350 g smoked mackerel
  fillet, skinned and
  flaked
6 spring onions or
  4 shallots, peeled
  and finely chopped
300 ml Bechamel Sauce
  (page 68)
salt
freshly ground black pepper
2 tomatoes, skinned and
  sliced
50 g Cheddar cheese,
  grated

Imperial
8 oz flour
pinch of salt
4 oz butter
1 egg, beaten

For the filling:
12 oz smoked mackerel
  fillet, skinned and
  flaked
6 spring onions or
  4 shallots, peeled
  and finely chopped
$\frac{1}{2}$ pint Bechamel Sauce
  (page 68)
salt
freshly ground black pepper
2 tomatoes, skinned and
  sliced
2 oz Cheddar cheese,
  grated

Cooking time: about 40 minutes
Oven: 200°C, 400°F, Gas Mark 6

Sift the flour and salt together into a bowl, then rub in the butter until the mixture resembles fine breadcrumbs. Mix to a light dough with the egg, wrap in cling film and chill for 10 minutes. Roll the pastry out on a lightly floured surface and line a 20 cm/8 inch flan ring. Bake blind in a preheated moderately hot oven for 20 minutes.
Mix together the fish, onion, sauce and salt and pepper to taste, then pour into the baked flan case. Arrange the tomato slices around the top and sprinkle with the cheese. Cook in the oven for 15 to 20 minutes or until golden and bubbling.

From left; Smoked fish platter;
Smoked fish fingers; Bloater crisp; Haddock soufflé

Smoked fish fingers

Metric
350 g smoked fish fillet
1 bay leaf
225 g potatoes, peeled
50 g butter
1 small onion, peeled
  and finely chopped
salt
freshly ground black pepper
2 eggs, beaten
50 g flour
100 g fresh white
  breadcrumbs
oil for deep frying
1 lemon, quartered,
  to garnish
Rémoulade Sauce (page
  74), to serve

Imperial
12 oz smoked fish fillet
1 bay leaf
8 oz potatoes, peeled
2 oz butter
1 small onion, peeled
  and finely chopped
salt
freshly ground black pepper
2 eggs, beaten
2 oz flour
4 oz fresh white
  breadcrumbs
oil for deep frying
1 lemon, quartered,
  to garnish
Rémoulade Sauce (page
  74), to serve

Cooking time: about 25 minutes

Put the fish in a pan, cover with water, add the bay leaf and poach for 10 minutes. Skin the fish and remove any bones, then flake the flesh. Boil the potatoes in salted water until tender. Drain well and mash with 25 g/1 oz of the butter. Melt the remaining butter in a pan and fry the onion until soft. Mix together the fish, potato, onion and salt and pepper to taste. Blend in half the beaten egg. Leave in a cool place for 15 to 20 minutes to firm up.
Shape the mixture into fingers, then coat in flour, beaten eggs and breadcrumbs. Heat the oil to 190°C/375°F and lower in half the fingers. Cook for 3 minutes or until golden, then drain on kitchen paper and keep warm while you cook the rest. Serve garnished with lemon and hand the sauce separately.

Smoked fish platter

Metric
1 × 225 g smoked trout,
  skinned and boned
4 × 5 cm pieces of
  smoked eel
4 thin slices of
  smoked salmon
1 small jar smoked
  mussels or oysters
large bunch of watercress
1 lemon, quartered,
  to garnish
150 ml Herb Mayonnaise
(page 75), to serve

Imperial
1 × 8 oz smoked trout,
  skinned and boned
4 × 2 inch pieces of
  smoked eel
4 thin slices of
  smoked salmon
1 small jar smoked
  mussels or oysters
large bunch of watercress
1 lemon, quartered,
  to garnish
¼ pint Herb Mayonnaise
  (page 75), to serve

As these smoked delicacies are so rich only a small amount of each is served. If you live near the sea use well washed seaweed instead of watercress to line the dish. If possible, serve the sauce in 4 large mussel shells or 1 scallop shell arranged in the centre of the dish.

Divide the trout into 4 fillets. Remove the skin and bone from the eel. Fold the salmon slices into four. Open and drain the mussels or oysters. Cover a large serving dish with watercress. Arrange the smoked fish decoratively. Garnish with lemon quarters and serve the sauce separately.

Variation:
Substitute smoked mackerel for the smoked trout.

56

Bloater crisp

Metric
4 × 175 g bloaters
4 × 5 ml spoons Dijon
mustard
1 small onion, peeled
and finely chopped
4 × 5 ml spoons chopped
fresh parsley
salt
freshly ground black pepper
4 × 15 ml spoons fresh
breadcrumbs
25 g butter
mustard and cress,
to garnish

Imperial
4 × 6 oz bloaters
4 teaspoons Dijon
mustard
1 small onion, peeled
and finely chopped
4 teaspoons chopped
fresh parsley
salt
freshly ground black pepper
4 tablespoons fresh
breadcrumbs
1 oz butter
mustard and cress,
to garnish

Cooking time: 20 minutes
Oven: 180°C, 350°F, Gas Mark 4

Split the fish and remove the backbone. Brush the insides with mustard, then sprinkle with onion, parsley, salt and pepper. Fold the fish over and lay in an ovenproof dish. Sprinkle with breadcrumbs and dot the butter over. Bake in a preheated moderate oven for 20 minutes. Serve from the dish, or arrange on a hot serving dish. Garnish with mustard and cress.

Variations:
Substitute smoked mackerel, cod, or golden cutlets for the haddock.

Haddock soufflé

Metric
225 g smoked haddock,
cooked, skinned and
flaked
50 g peeled prawns
25 g butter
25 g flour
200 ml milk
squeeze of lemon juice
salt
freshly ground black pepper
3 large eggs, separated
15 g grated Parmesan
cheese

Imperial
8 oz smoked haddock,
cooked, skinned and
flaked
2 oz peeled prawns
1 oz butter
1 oz flour
⅓ pint milk
squeeze of lemon juice
salt
freshly ground black pepper
3 large eggs, separated
½ oz grated Parmesan
cheese

Cooking time: about 35 minutes
Oven: 190°C, 375°F, Gas Mark 5

Mix the haddock with the prawns. Melt the butter in a pan, stir in the flour and cook for 1 minute. Remove from the heat and gradually blend in the milk, lemon juice and salt and pepper to taste. Return to the heat and cook gently, stirring, until the sauce is thick and smooth. Remove from the heat, then stir in the egg yolks and fish, mixing well together. Beat the egg whites with a few grains of salt until stiff, then fold carefully into the fish mixture.
Butter a 18 cm/7 inch soufflé dish and dust the inside with the cheese. Pour in the mixture and bake in the centre of a preheated moderately hot oven for 25 minutes or until well risen and golden. Serve at once.

57

Smothered herrings à la russe; Swedish finnan

Swedish finnan

Metric	Imperial
225 g smoked haddock fillet, skinned and boned	8 oz smoked haddock fillet, skinned and boned
4 medium potatoes, peeled and thinly sliced	4 medium potatoes, peeled and thinly sliced
4 tomatoes, skinned and sliced	4 tomatoes, skinned and sliced
freshly ground black pepper	freshly ground black pepper
2 × 5 ml spoons anchovy essence	2 teaspoons anchovy essence
2 large eggs	2 large eggs
300 ml milk	½ pint milk
25 g butter	1 oz butter

Cooking time: about 45 minutes
Oven: 160°C, 325°F, Gas Mark 3

Flake the haddock flesh. Butter an ovenproof serving dish and layer the potatoes, fish and tomatoes in it, seasoning with black pepper to taste. Finish with a layer of overlapping slices of potato. Beat the anchovy essence into the eggs with the milk and season with black pepper. Pour carefully into the dish. Dot over the butter. Bake in a preheated moderate oven for 45 minutes or until the potatoes are tender and the top is golden brown.

Smothered herrings à la russe

Metric	Imperial
4 soused herrings (page 29)	4 soused herrings (page 29)
300 ml soured cream	½ pint soured cream
4 spring onions, finely chopped	4 spring onions, finely chopped
1 eating apple, cored and sliced	1 eating apple, cored and sliced
50 g pickled beetroot, diced	2 oz pickled beetroot, diced
salt	salt
freshly ground black pepper	freshly ground black pepper
To garnish:	To garnish:
few toasted walnut halves	few toasted walnut halves
chopped fresh parsley	chopped fresh parsley

Drain and remove the head, tail and backbone of the herrings. Lay them in a serving dish. Lightly whip the cream and fold in the onion, apple and beetroot, which will turn the cream a pleasing pink. Add a very little of the beet liquor if the colour is not deep enough. Add salt and pepper to taste. Pour over the fish and garnish with walnuts and parsley.

Variation:
Substitute plain yogurt for the soured cream.

58

Omelette Arnold Bennett

Metric	Imperial
225 g cooked, flaked smoked haddock	8 oz cooked, flaked smoked haddock
3 × 15 ml spoons grated Parmesan cheese	3 tablespoons grated Parmesan cheese
salt	salt
freshly ground black pepper	freshly ground black pepper
25 g butter	1 oz butter
6 eggs, lightly beaten	6 eggs, lightly beaten
4 × 15 ml spoons double cream	4 tablespoons double cream
4 sprigs of watercress, to garnish	4 sprigs of watercress, to garnish

Cooking time: 6 to 7 minutes

Haddock is essential for this dish, no other smoked fish will give the unique flavour. To serve 4 people, double the ingredients and make 2 omelettes.

Mix together the fish, 2 × 15 ml spoons/2 tablespoons of the cheese, and salt and pepper. Heat the butter in a large frying pan, then pour in the eggs. Shake the pan gently and stir the eggs with the back of a fork until they begin to set – a few moments. Remove from the heat, then spread the fish on top of the eggs. Stir the remaining cheese into the cream and pour over the mixture. Place under a hot grill and cook until lightly coloured and bubbling. Slide, unfolded, on to a hot serving dish and garnish with watercress.

Serves 2

Omelette Arnold Bennett

SOUPS & STEWS

Over the last few years fish soups have gained an importance in our kitchens, the fish stew, however, is slower to gain popularity. Perhaps it is the very name fish stew which does not have the romantic sound of cioppino, bouillabaisse, matelote or chowder. Nevertheless they have excellent ingredients and many of these recipes, accompanied by plenty of good crusty French bread need only be followed by a little fresh fruit and/or cheese.

Soup makes good use of left over fish, and a can of tuna or salmon can provide a good cream soup.

Bisque is rightfully the name of soup made with shellfish, although it is now used for many thickened fish soups. The delicious and lightly flavoured court bouillon used for poaching fish should never be thrown away, it can form the basis of many different soups and stews.

Court bouillon

Metric	Imperial
2¼ litres water	2 pints water
500 g carrots, peeled and sliced	1 lb carrots, peeled and sliced
2 onions, peeled and sliced	2 onions, peeled and sliced
bouquet garni	bouquet garni
1 × 15 ml spoon salt	1 tablespoon salt
12 peppercorns	12 peppercorns
bunch of parsley stalks, roughly chopped	bunch of parsley stalks, roughly chopped
150 ml wine vinegar	¼ pint wine vinegar

Cooking time: 45 minutes

Whole, large pieces of fish and shellfish are usually poached in a flavoured liquid, known as court bouillon. This is made up, then allowed to become cold before use. It can be strained and used several times if kept chilled.

Place all the ingredients in a large pan, bring to the boil and simmer for 45 minutes. Strain, then cool the liquid.

White wine court bouillon

Metric
600 ml dry white wine
600 ml water
2 × 5 ml spoons salt
1 onion, peeled and sliced
1 carrot, peeled and sliced
6 peppercorns
1 bay leaf
6 parsley stalks, or
    small bunch of parsley,
    roughly chopped
sprig of thyme
2 cloves

Imperial
1 pint dry white wine
1 pint water
2 teaspoons salt
1 onion, peeled and sliced
1 carrot, peeled and sliced
6 peppercorns
1 bay leaf
6 parsley stalks, or
    small bunch of parsley,
    roughly chopped
sprig of thyme
2 cloves

Cooking time: 30 minutes

Some recipes may call for a court bouillon made with white wine, especially if it is to be used as part of the sauce.

Place all the ingredients in a large pan, bring to the boil and simmer for 30 minutes. Strain, then cool the liquid.

Far left and right: stages of making Fish stock
Centre: Court bouillon

Fish stock

Metric
1 kg raw fish bones,
    heads and trimmings
1 onion, peeled and
    sliced
1 carrot, peeled and sliced
½ celery stick, sliced
12 peppercorns
1 bay leaf
1 × 15 ml spoon white
    wine vinegar
strip of lemon rind
150 ml dry white wine
pinch of salt

Imperial
2 lb raw fish bones,
    heads and trimmings
1 onion, peeled and
    sliced
1 carrot, peeled and sliced
½ celery stick, sliced
12 peppercorns
1 bay leaf
1 tablespoon white
    wine vinegar
strip of lemon rind
¼ pint dry white wine
pinch of salt

Cooking time: 25 minutes

A good fish stock is essential to the flavouring of sauces for fish. However, not all fish bones and trimmings will give flavour – ask for Dover sole, whiting, turbot or witch, as plaice and lemon sole are practically tasteless.

Rinse the trimmings and break them up. Butter a large saucepan, put in the fish, onion, carrot and celery. Cover and cook over a gentle heat for 5 minutes. Uncover and add the remaining ingredients, bring to the boil, then simmer for 20 minutes only. The bones render a bitterness if cooked for too long. Strain, then cool the liquid quickly. If a stronger stock is needed, reduce the strained liquid by rapid boiling to half the quantity. This will set like a jelly when cold.

Scandinavian salmon soup

Metric	Imperial
50 g long grain rice	2 oz long grain rice
the head of a large salmon, washed	the head of a large salmon, washed
1.2 litres Fish Stock (page 61)	2 pints Fish Stock (page 61)
1 onion, peeled and sliced	1 onion, peeled and sliced
2 carrots, peeled and sliced	2 carrots, peeled and sliced
1 celery stick, sliced	1 celery stick, sliced
1 × 2.5 ml spoon dill seeds	½ teaspoon dill seeds
salt	salt
freshly ground black pepper	freshly ground black pepper
2 × 15 ml spoons double cream (optional)	2 tablespoons double cream (optional)

To garnish:
few peeled shrimps
chopped fresh dill or
  parsley

To garnish:
few peeled shrimps
chopped fresh dill or
  parsley

Cooking time: about 1 hour

A friendly fishmonger will let you have a large salmon head relatively cheaply. Rye bread goes well with this impressive soup.

Put the rice in a strainer, rinse well, then leave to drain. Place the salmon head in a large pan and pour in the stock. Bring to the boil, reduce the heat, then simmer gently for 20 minutes. Remove the head on to a dish. Strain the liquid into a clean pan, then add the rice, onion, carrots, celery, dill seeds and salt and pepper to taste. Bring to the boil, reduce the heat, then simmer for about 20 minutes, or until the rice and vegetables are tender.

Meanwhile, pick the flesh from the fish head and add to the soup with the cream (if using). Reheat gently, then taste and adjust the seasoning. Pour into a heated tureen or individual soup dishes and garnish with shrimps and dill.

Haddie chowder

Metric	Imperial
500 g finnan haddock fillet	1 lb finnan haddock fillet
50 g butter	2 oz butter
2 large onions, peeled and and chopped	2 large onions, peeled and and chopped
4 medium potatoes, peeled and sliced	4 medium potatoes, peeled and sliced
2 celery sticks, finely sliced	2 celery sticks, finely sliced
1 bay leaf	1 bay leaf
1 garlic clove, peeled and crushed	1 garlic clove, peeled and crushed
1 × 2.5 ml spoon paprika	½ teaspoon paprika
1 × 15 ml spoon chopped fresh parsley	1 tablespoon chopped fresh parsley
salt	salt
freshly ground black pepper	freshly ground black pepper
2 × 15 ml spoons quick porridge oats	2 tablespoons quick porridge oats
450 g hot milk	¾ pint hot milk
8 × 5 ml spoons sherry	8 teaspoons sherry
few spring onions, finely sliced, to garnish	few spring onions, finely sliced, to garnish

Crab chowder

Metric	Imperial
50 g butter	2 oz butter
1 large onion, peeled and finely sliced	1 large onion, peeled and finely sliced
500 g ripe tomatoes, skinned, seeded and chopped	1 lb ripe tomatoes, skinned, seeded and chopped
900 ml chicken stock	1½ pints chicken stock
sprig of thyme	sprig of thyme
1 × 400 g can of corn kernels, drained	1 × 14 oz can of corn kernels, drained
500 g crab meat	1 lb crab meat
few drops of Tabasco	few drops of Tabasco
salt	salt
freshly ground black pepper	freshly ground black pepper
chopped fresh chervil or parsley, to garnish	chopped fresh chervil or parsley, to garnish

Cooking time: about 20 minutes

Melt the butter, add the onion and fry until soft. Add the tomatoes, then cover and stew gently for 10 minutes. Add the stock, thyme, corn kernels, crab meat, Tabasco and salt and pepper to taste. Cover the pan, then simmer for 5 minutes. Turn into a heated tureen or individual soup dishes and sprinkle with chervil or parsley.

Scandinavian salmon soup

Cooking time: 35 minutes

Hot garlic bread is very good with this.

Place the haddock in a heat resistant dish, then pour over enough boiling water to cover. Leave for 3 minutes, then drain and reserve the liquid. Skin and flake the fish. Melt the butter in a pan, add the onions and fry until soft. Add the fish, potatoes, 300 ml/½ pint of the reserved liquor, celery, bay leaf, garlic, paprika, parsley and salt and pepper to taste. Simmer gently for about 20 minutes, or until the potatoes are tender.
Stir in the oats and hot milk, taste and adjust the seasoning, then simmer for a further 5 minutes. Pour directly into hot soup dishes and stir 2 × 5 ml spoons/ 2 teaspoons of sherry into each one. Sprinkle with the onion and serve at once.

From front: Crab chowder; Haddie chowder

Bourride

Cooking time: about 20 minutes
Oven: 180°C, 350°F, Gas Mark 4

Metric
750 g witch fillet
*900 ml Fish Stock (page
   61)*
3 egg yolks
150 ml double cream
salt
freshly ground black pepper
squeeze of lemon juice
*4 slices French bread,
   brushed with olive
   oil and baked until crisp*
150 ml garlic mayonnaise

Imperial
1½ lb witch fillet
*1½ pints Fish Stock (page
   61)*
3 egg yolks
¼ pint double cream
salt
freshly ground black pepper
squeeze of lemon juice
*4 slices French bread,
   brushed with olive
   oil and baked until crisp*
¼ pint garlic mayonnaise

This Provençale fish soup with garlic mayonnaise is a substantial dish.

Rinse the fish and cut into 4 portions. Place in a buttered ovenproof dish, moisten with about 150 ml/¼ pint of the fish stock, then poach in a preheated moderate oven for 15 minutes.
Mix together the egg yolks and cream and add salt and pepper. Whisk into the remaining fish stock in a pan and reheat thoroughly, stirring, but do not allow it to boil. Taste and adjust the seasoning, then add the lemon juice and the liquor from the poached fish.
To serve, place a croûte of bread in each heated soup dish. Arrange the fish portions on top and pour over the soup. Mask the fish with the mayonnaise and serve immediately.

From right: Halibut soup with saffron; Bourride; Matelote of eel

Matelote of eel

Metric	Imperial
1 kg of eel, skinned and cleaned	2 lb of eel, skinned and cleaned
2 onions, peeled and chopped	2 onions, peeled and chopped
4 shallots, peeled and chopped	4 shallots, peeled and chopped
1 garlic clove, peeled and crushed	1 garlic clove, peeled and crushed
salt	salt
freshly ground black pepper	freshly ground black pepper
bouquet garni	bouquet garni
sprig of tarragon	sprig of tarragon
2 × 15 ml spoons brandy (optional)	2 tablespoons brandy (optional)
1 bottle of red burgundy	1 bottle of red burgundy
75 g butter	3 oz butter
12 button onions, peeled	12 button onions, peeled
12 mushrooms, wiped	12 mushrooms, wiped
15 g flour	½ oz flour
1 × 5 ml spoon meat extract	1 teaspoon meat extract

To garnish:	To garnish:
circles of fried bread	circles of fried bread
chopped fresh parsley	chopped fresh parsley

Cooking time: 50 to 60 minutes

This very robust dish is a French stew.

Cut the eel into 7½ cm/3 inch pieces. Grease the bottom of a thick pan and lay the onions, shallots, garlic and eel in it, season lightly with salt and pepper then add the bouquet garni and tarragon sprig. Cover the pan, place over a gentle heat and cook for 10 minutes. If using brandy, warm it slightly, pour over the eel and ignite. When the flames subside pour in the wine, then cover and simmer for 20 minutes. Meanwhile, melt 25 g/1 oz of the butter in a pan, add the button onions and cook for 5 minutes, then add the mushrooms and cook for a further 5 minutes. When the eel is tender lift it into the mushroom pan and keep warm. Remove and discard the bouquet garni. Reduce the wine by boiling rapidly to half the original amount, then remove from the heat. Cream the remaining butter with the flour and stir into the wine mixture. Return the pan to the heat and simmer for 5 minutes. Stir in the meat extract to deepen the colour (red wine loses its colour in cooking, which can look unappetizing). Place the eel and vegetables in a deep hot serving dish and pour the sauce over. Garnish with the bread rounds, one half of each dipped in chopped parsley.

Halibut soup with saffron

Metric	Imperial
500 g halibut	1 lb halibut
300 ml White Wine Court Bouillon (page 61)	½ pint White Wine Court Bouillon (page 61)
50 g butter	2 oz butter
1 onion, peeled and chopped	1 onion, peeled and chopped
1 garlic clove, peeled and crushed	1 garlic clove, peeled and crushed
225 g ripe tomatoes, skinned, seeded and chopped	8 oz ripe tomatoes, skinned, seeded and chopped
1 × 15 ml spoon chopped fresh parsley	1 tablespoon chopped fresh parsley
1 × 15 ml spoon chopped fresh chives	1 tablespoon chopped fresh chives
sprig of thyme	sprig of thyme
1 bay leaf	1 bay leaf
pinch of ground mace or nutmeg	pinch of ground mace or nutmeg
pinch of saffron, steeped in 2 × 5 ml spoons boiling water	pinch of saffron, steeped in 2 teaspoons boiling water
salt	salt
freshly ground black pepper	freshly ground black pepper
300 ml milk	½ pint milk
300 ml single cream	½ pint single cream
1 red pepper, fresh or canned, diced, to garnish	1 red pepper, fresh or canned, diced, to garnish
Watercress Butter (page 79), to serve	Watercress Butter (page 79), to serve

Cooking time: about 30 minutes

Any white fish, such as cod, hake or monkfish could be used instead of halibut for this soup.

Rinse the fish and cut into 4 pieces, then place in a pan and just cover with the court bouillon. Cover and bring to the boil, then reduce the heat and poach for 8 minutes.
Melt the butter in a pan, add the onion and garlic and fry gently until soft and golden. Add the tomatoes, parsley, chives, thyme, bay leaf, mace or nutmeg, saffron and salt and pepper to taste.
Remove any bones and skin from the fish. Strain the poaching liquid into the tomato mixture, then add the fish flesh. Simmer gently for 15 to 20 minutes. Remove from the heat, stir in the milk and cream, taste and adjust the seasoning, then simmer for 5 minutes. Pour into heated soup dishes with a portion of fish in each one. Garnish with red pepper and serve with hot toast and watercress butter.

Cream of mussel soup

Metric	Imperial
1 kg mussels, scrubbed and cleaned	2 lb mussels, scrubbed and cleaned
150 ml dry white wine	$\frac{1}{4}$ pint dry white wine
150 ml water	$\frac{1}{4}$ pint water
1 onion, peeled and finely chopped	1 onion, peeled and finely chopped
1 celery stick, finely chopped	1 celery stick, finely chopped
bouquet garni	bouquet garni
1 clove	1 clove
6 peppercorns	6 peppercorns
salt	salt
300 ml Bechamel Sauce (page 68)	$\frac{1}{2}$ pint Bechamel Sauce (page 68)
250 ml single cream	8 fl oz single cream
pinch of cayenne	pinch of cayenne
pinch of nutmeg	pinch of nutmeg
chopped fresh chervil or parsley, to garnish	chopped fresh chervil or parsley, to garnish

Cooking time: about 20 minutes

Put the mussels in a large pan with the wine, water, onion, celery, bouquet garni, clove and peppercorns. Cover and place over a low heat until the mussels open. Shake the pan once or twice. Strain the liquid into a basin, leave for 5 minutes, then strain again through double muslin into a saucepan. This is to remove any trace of sand there may be. Add a little salt and the béchamel sauce to the pan, bring to the boil, then remove from the heat. Stir in the cream and season to taste with salt, cayenne and nutmeg.

Pick the mussels from the shells, add them to the soup and reheat very carefully. Do not allow the soup to boil – this will toughen the mussels. Pour into heated soup dishes and garnish with chervil or parsley.

Right: Crème cardinale
Below: Cream of mussel soup

Crème cardinale

Cooking time: about 1 hour
Oven: 180°C, 350°F, Gas Mark 4

Metric
1 × 500 g lobster, cooked
40 g butter
1 onion, peeled and sliced
1 carrot, peeled and sliced
1 celery stick, sliced
25 g flour
600 ml milk
cayenne
salt
freshly ground black pepper
2 egg yolks
150 ml double cream
2 × 15 ml spoons
   brandy (optional)
2 × 15 ml spoons dry sherry
small jar of Danish lump
   fish roe, to garnish
   (optional)

Imperial
1 × 1 lb lobster, cooked
1½ oz butter
1 onion, peeled and sliced
1 carrot, peeled and sliced
1 celery stick, sliced
1 oz flour
1 pint milk
cayenne
salt
freshly ground black pepper
2 egg yolks
¼ pint double cream
2 tablespoons
   brandy (optional)
2 tablespoons dry sherry
small jar of Danish lump
   fish roe, to garnish
   (optional)

Remove all the meat from the lobster shell, dice and reserve it. Place the shell in a preheated moderate oven for 20 minutes to dry out. Pound the shell as finely as possible. Melt the butter in a pan and add the shell, onion, carrot and celery. Cover and cook for 20 minutes over a very low heat, do not allow it to burn. Stir in the flour and cook for a minute. Remove the pan from the heat and blend in the milk, a little cayenne and salt and pepper to taste.

Return to the heat, then simmer for 20 minutes. Strain the sauce through a double muslin, then return it to the pan.

Beat the egg yolks with the cream, add a ladleful of the soup, then pour the mixture into the pan. Reheat gently, stirring, until it thickens slightly, on no account allow it to boil. Add the lobster meat, brandy (if using) and the sherry. Taste and adjust the seasoning, reheat if necessary, and serve in heated soup dishes garnished with 1 × 5 ml spoon/1 teaspoon of lump fish roe, if liked.

SAUCES & BUTTERS

A good sauce cannot be made in a hurry. Reduction of the liquid to be thickened is of first importance. You may be left with 600 ml/ 1 pint of poaching liquid and all you need is 150 ml/¼ pint of finished sauce. Concentrate the flavour of the liquid by boiling it rapidly until reduced to the required amount, then proceed.

There are, however, a few short cuts. To one basic sauce (known as the mother sauce) various additions can be made to produce many other sauces. Bechamel is one example, mayonnaise another.

The usual method of thickening sauces is by using a roux, a mixture of butter and flour. These are cooked gently together before the liquid is added, a little at a time, until it is all absorbed. The sauce must be constantly stirred as it is brought to the boil.

Savoury butters are used with grilled and fried fish in place of a sauce, but there are recipes which call for a flavoured butter to be whisked into a finished sauce or soup, for example, lobster butter to lobster bisque.

Personal choice is important: because a recipe suggests cheese sauce as an accompaniment it does not mean that this is the only one suitable – serve the sauce of your preference and bring your own ideas into your cooking.

Bechamel sauce

Metric	Imperial
600 ml milk	1 pint milk
1 small onion, peeled and quartered	1 small onion, peeled and quartered
1 bay leaf	1 bay leaf
2 cloves	2 cloves
1 small carrot, peeled and quartered	1 small carrot, peeled and quartered
2 mace blades or good pinch of ground mace	2 mace blades or good pinch of ground mace
2 small slices of celery	2 small slices of celery
12 peppercorns	12 peppercorns
50 g butter	2 oz butter
50 g flour	2 oz flour
salt	salt

Cooking time: about 35 minutes

A well flavoured bechamel sauce is the foundation for a great number of sauces, which will add variety to your cooking. You can safely make more than you need as it keeps, well covered, in the refrigerator for a week.

Pour the milk into a pan, then add the onion, bay leaf, cloves, carrot, mace, celery and peppercorns. Cover and bring very slowly to the boil, then simmer for 3 minutes. Remove from the heat and leave for 20 minutes, to allow the flavours to infuse.

Melt the butter in another pan, stir in the flour and cook gently, stirring, for 5 minutes. Do not allow it to colour. Remove from the heat. Strain the milk and gradually stir it into the roux. Bring to the boil and add salt to taste. Simmer for 10 minutes, then taste and adjust the seasoning.

Variations using 300 ml/½ pint bechamel sauce :

Anchovy Sauce: Bring the bechamel sauce to the boil, stir in 2 × 5 ml spoons/2 teaspoons anchovy essence (a little more can be added if liked) and a squeeze of lemon juice. Add salt and pepper to taste. Serve with baked, poached, grilled or fried white or oily fish and fish fingers.

Cheese Sauce: Stir 1 × 2.5 ml spoon/½ teaspoon dry mustard into the bechamel sauce and bring to the boil. Remove from the heat and stir in 2 × 15 ml spoons/ 2 tablespoons grated Cheddar cheese until it melts. Add salt and pepper to taste. Layer the sauce with cooked white or smoked fish, prawns, etc, sprinkle with extra cheese and breadcrumbs, grill quickly and serve hot.

Mushroom Sauce: Melt 15 g/½ oz butter, add the juice of half a lemon and 50 g/2 oz finely sliced mushrooms. Cook over a gentle heat for 3 to 4 minutes. Bring the bechamel sauce to the boil, add the mushrooms and juice from the pan, then add salt and pepper to taste. Serve with poached white fish, fish soufflés and fish moulds.

From left: The first stage in making Bechamel sauce.
Variations: Anchovy sauce; Cheese sauce; Mushroom sauce

Tarragon cream dressing

Metric	Imperial
1 egg yolk	1 egg yolk
1 × 2.5 ml spoon chopped fresh tarragon or pinch of dried tarragon	½ teaspoon chopped fresh tarragon or pinch of dried tarragon
150 ml soured cream	¼ pint soured cream
1 × 5 ml spoon sugar	1 teaspoon sugar
little crushed garlic	little crushed garlic
2 × 5 ml spoons wine vinegar	2 teaspoons wine vinegar
salt	salt
freshly ground black pepper	freshly ground black pepper

Cooking time: 4 to 5 minutes

Serve with fish salads, cocktails and mousses.

Beat together the egg yolk and tarragon in a bowl. Stir in the cream, sugar and garlic. Place the bowl over hot water and cook gently, stirring, until it thickens. Remove from the heat, stir in the vinegar and add salt and pepper to taste. Chill.

White wine sauce

Metric	Imperial
4 × 15 ml spoons dry white wine	4 tablespoons dry white wine
1 shallot, peeled and chopped	1 shallot, peeled and chopped
1 mace blade	1 mace blade
½ bay leaf	½ bay leaf
25 g butter	1 oz butter
15 g flour	1 oz flour
150 ml Fish Stock (page 61)	¼ pint Fish Stock (page 61)
4 × 15 ml spoons milk	4 tablespoons milk
salt	salt
freshly ground black pepper	freshly ground black pepper

Cooking time: about 20 minutes

This sauce is solely for fish. It goes particularly well with white fish such as poached plaice, turbot and brill.

Put the wine in a small pan, add the shallot, mace and bay leaf. Bring to the boil and simmer until reduced by half. Set aside.
Melt the butter in a pan, then stir in the flour and cook for 1 minute. Remove from the heat and blend in the fish stock and strain in the wine. Bring to the boil, then simmer very gently for 10 minutes. Add the milk, bring to the boil for 2 minutes and add salt and pepper to taste.

Niçoise sauce

Metric	Imperial
1 × 15 ml spoon tomato purée	*1 tablespoon tomato purée*
300 ml mayonnaise	*½ pint mayonnaise*
1 green or red pepper, cored, seeded and finely chopped	*1 green or red pepper, cored, seeded and finely chopped*
1 × 5 ml spoon chopped fresh tarragon or pinch of dried tarragon	*1 teaspoon chopped fresh tarragon or pinch of dried tarragon*
1 × 5 ml spoon chopped chives	*1 teaspoon chopped chives*
1 garlic clove, peeled and crushed	*1 garlic clove, peeled and crushed*
salt	*salt*
freshly ground black pepper	*freshly ground black pepper*

Serve with fish and shellfish salads, grilled and fried white fish and deep-fried scampi.

Put the tomato purée into a small bowl and stir in 1 × 15 ml spoon/1 tablespoon of the mayonnaise. Fold into the mayonnaise with the remaining ingredients. Add salt and pepper to taste.

Apple and horseradish sauce

Metric	Imperial
500 g cooking apples, roughly chopped	*1 lb cooking apples, roughly chopped*
2 × 15 ml spoons water	*2 tablespoons water*
2 cloves	*2 cloves*
50 g sugar	*2 oz sugar*
25 g butter	*1 oz butter*
squeeze of lemon juice	*squeeze of lemon juice*
2 × 15 ml spoons grated horseradish or bottled horseradish sauce	*2 tablespoons grated horseradish or bottled horseradish sauce*

Cooking time: 15 minutes

The acidity of this sauce counteracts the richness of fried, grilled or baked oily fish. It also gives a lift to poached white fish such as cod, coley and haddock.

Place the apples in a pan with the water, cloves and sugar. Simmer until tender, then rub through a sieve. Stir in the butter, lemon juice and horseradish and reheat gently.

Scandinavian mustard sauce

Metric	Imperial
2 × 15 ml spoons Dijon mustard	*2 tablespoons Dijon mustard*
1 × 15 ml spoon caster sugar	*1 tablespoon caster sugar*
1 egg yolk	*1 egg yolk*
2 × 15 ml spoons white wine vinegar	*2 tablespoons white wine vinegar*
7 × 15 ml spoons salad oil	*7 tablespoons salad oil*
salt	*salt*
freshly ground black pepper	*freshly ground black pepper*
3 × 15 ml spoons chopped dill or fennel	*3 tablespoons chopped dill or fennel*

This goes well with cold boiled lobster and crab, and fish salads.

Mix the mustard, sugar, egg yolk and vinegar together. Slowly whisk in the oil to form an emulsion. Add salt and pepper to taste, then stir in the dill or fennel.

From front: Tarragon cream dressing; Scandinavian mustard sauce; Apple and horseradish sauce; White wine sauce; Niçoise sauce

Prince's sauce

Metric	Imperial
25 g mixed fresh herbs e.g. parsley, tarragon, chives, marjoram	1 oz mixed fresh herbs e.g. parsley, tarragon, chives, marjoram
3 anchovy fillets	3 anchovy fillets
3 yolks of hard-boiled eggs	3 yolks of hard-boiled eggs
2 × 5 ml spoons dry mustard	2 teaspoons dry mustard
1 × 5 ml spoon capers	1 teaspoon capers
4 × 15 ml spoons olive or salad oil	4 tablespoons olive or salad oil
freshly ground black pepper	freshly ground black pepper

Cooking time: 3 to 4 minutes

The leftover egg whites from the hard-boiled eggs can be sliced and used in a salad. Serve with fish salads and grilled or fried white fish.

Bring a small pan of water to the boil and add the herbs. Cook for 3 minutes, then drain and dab dry on kitchen paper. Pound the anchovies with the egg yolks, adding the mustard, capers and herbs. When well mixed, whisk in the oil. Add pepper to taste. Rub through a fine sieve and chill.

Fresh tomato sauce

Metric	Imperial
2 × 15 ml spoons oil	2 tablespoons oil
1 large garlic clove, peeled and crushed	1 large garlic clove, peeled and crushed
1 large onion, peeled and finely chopped	1 large onion, peeled and finely chopped
½ green pepper, cored, seeded and finely chopped	½ green pepper, cored, seeded and finely chopped
500 g ripe tomatoes, halved	1 lb ripe tomatoes, halved
1 bay leaf	1 bay leaf
½ celery stick, sliced	½ celery stick, sliced
sprig of thyme	sprig of thyme
salt	salt
freshly ground black pepper	freshly ground black pepper

Cooking time: about 50 minutes

Serve with poached, grilled, fried or baked white or oily fish, with the exception of the salmon family.

Heat the oil in a large pan, add the garlic, onion and pepper and cook gently until they begin to colour. Add the remaining ingredients, then simmer for 45 minutes or until thick. Rub through a fine sieve, return to the pan, reheat and taste and adjust the seasoning.

Fish velouté sauce

Metric	Imperial
50 g butter	2 oz butter
12 peppercorns	12 peppercorns
few parsley stalks	few parsley stalks
25 g mushrooms, sliced	1 oz mushrooms, sliced
50 g flour	2 oz flour
600 ml Fish Stock (page 61)	1 pint Fish Stock (page 61)
juice of ½ lemon	juice of ½ lemon
salt	salt
freshly ground black pepper	freshly ground black pepper
2 × 15 ml spoons double cream (optional)	2 tablespoons double cream (optional)

Cooking time: 20 minutes

Serve with poached white or oily fish, plain or flavoured in much the same way as for bechamel.

Melt the butter in a pan, add the peppercorns, parsley stalks and mushrooms and cook gently for 5 minutes. Stir in the flour and cook for another 2 minutes. Remove from the heat and gradually stir in the stock. Return to the heat and bring slowly to the boil, stirring. Reduce the heat, then simmer gently for 10 minutes. Strain the sauce, add the lemon juice and salt and pepper to taste. Stir in the cream, if using. Taste and adjust the seasoning.

Prince's sauce; Fresh tomato sauce

Sauce smitaine

Metric
1 × 15 ml spoon butter
1 medium onion, peeled
    and sliced
120 ml dry white wine
250 ml soured cream
salt
freshly ground black pepper
lemon juice to taste

Imperial
1 tablespoon butter
1 medium onion, peeled
    and sliced
4 fl oz dry white wine
8 fl oz soured cream
salt
freshly ground black pepper
lemon juice to taste

Cooking time: about 20 minutes

Melt the butter in a pan, add the onion and cook gently until soft. Add the wine and reduce by boiling over a medium heat to 2 × 5 ml spoons/2 teaspoons. In another pan, bring the cream to scalding point, then stir into the wine. Simmer for 5 minutes. Strain through a fine sieve, return to the pan, reheat and add salt, pepper and lemon juice to taste.

From front: Fish velouté sauce; Sauce smitaine

Left: Curried apricot sauce; Front: Rémoulade sauce; Back: Herb mayonnaise

Rémoulade sauce

Metric	Imperial
300 ml mayonnaise	½ pint mayonnaise
1 × 15 ml spoon finely chopped gherkins	1 tablespoon finely chopped gherkins
1 × 5 ml spoon Dijon mustard	1 teaspoon Dijon mustard
1 × 5 ml spoon chopped capers	1 teaspoon chopped capers
1 × 5 ml spoon chopped fresh chervil or pinch of dried chervil	1 teaspoon chopped fresh chervil or pinch of dried chervil
1 × 5 ml spoon chopped fresh parsley or pinch of dried parsley	1 teaspoon chopped fresh parsley or pinch of dried parsley
1 × 5 ml spoon chopped fresh tarragon or pinch of dried tarragon	1 teaspoon chopped fresh tarragon or pinch of dried tarragon
1 × 2.5 ml spoon anchovy essence	½ teaspoon anchovy essence

Serve with fish and shellfish salads and fish mousses.

Put the mayonnaise into a mixing bowl and fold in the remaining ingredients.

Curried apricot mayonnaise

Metric	Imperial
300 ml mayonnaise	½ pint mayonnaise
1 × 5 ml spoon curry paste	1 teaspoon curry paste
1 × 15 ml spoon good apricot jam	1 tablespoon good apricot jam
squeeze of lemon juice	squeeze of lemon juice

Hand a bowl of this mayonnaise as an accompaniment to cold poached white fish and shellfish salads.

In a small bowl mix together 1 × 15 ml spoon/1 tablespoon of the mayonnaise, the curry paste and jam. Beat until well blended, then fold into the mayonnaise.

Herb mayonnaise

<table>
<tr><td>Metric</td><td>Imperial</td></tr>
</table>

Metric
*2 × 15 ml spoons chopped
  fresh basil or 1 × 15 ml
  spoon dried basil*
*2 × 15 ml spoons chopped
  fresh parsley*
*2 × 15 ml spoons chopped
  shallot*
2 eggs
*1 × 15 ml spoon tarragon
  vinegar*
*1 × 5 ml spoon Dijon
  mustard*
salt
freshly ground black pepper
300 ml olive or salad oil
*3 × 15 ml spoons double
  cream*

Imperial
*2 tablespoons chopped
  fresh basil or 1
  tablespoon dried basil*
*2 tablespoons chopped
  fresh parsley*
*2 tablespoons chopped
  shallot*
2 eggs
*1 tablespoon tarragon
  vinegar*
*1 teaspoon Dijon
  mustard*
salt
freshly ground black pepper
½ pint olive or salad oil
*3 tablespoons double
  cream*

This herb mayonnaise differs from the usual one in that the whole eggs are very lightly cooked, and it is flavoured with shallot. It is best made in a liquidizer. Serve with fish and shellfish cocktails and mousses.

Bring a small pan of water to the boil, add the herbs and shallot and cook for 30 seconds. Drain and dab dry on kitchen paper. Simmer the eggs in water for 3 minutes. Break the eggs into the liquidizer goblet, then add the herb mixture, vinegar, mustard and salt and pepper to taste. Blend at high speed for 1 minute, then, still at high speed, pour in the oil in a steady steam. Switch the motor to low and add the cream. Transfer the mayonnaise to a bowl and taste and adjust the seasoning. Chill.

Mickeval fish devil

Metric
100 g butter
*2 × 15 ml spoons tomato
  ketchup*
*1 × 15 ml spoon
  Worcestershire sauce*
1 onion, peeled and grated
*1 × 5 ml spoon made
  mustard*
*1 garlic clove, peeled and
  crushed*
*2 × 5 ml spoons chopped
  fresh parsley*
*1 × 5 ml spoon chopped
  fresh tarragon, or pinch
  of dried*
few drops of Tabasco
salt

Imperial
4 oz butter
*2 tablespoons tomato
  ketchup*
*1 tablespoon
  Worcestershire sauce*
1 onion, peeled and grated
*1 teaspoon made
  mustard*
*1 garlic clove, peeled and
  crushed*
*2 teaspoons chopped
  fresh parsley*
*1 teaspoon chopped
  fresh tarragon, or pinch
  of dried*
few drops of Tabasco
salt

Cooking time: 5 minutes

Serve chilled with grilled fish.

In a small pan melt the butter gently. Stir in the remaining ingredients except the Tabasco and salt. Bring to the boil, remove from the heat and add Tabasco and salt to taste.

Tomato mayonnaise

Metric
*225 g ripe tomatoes,
  skinned, seeded and
  diced*
*2 × 5 ml spoons tomato
  purée*
*1 × 15 ml spoon chopped
  fresh basil or 1 × 5 ml
  spoon dried*
300 ml mayonnaise
salt
freshly ground black pepper

Imperial
*8 oz ripe tomatoes,
  skinned, seeded and
  diced*
*2 teaspoons tomato
  purée*
*1 tablespoon chopped
  fresh basil or 1 teaspoon
  dried*
½ pint mayonnaise
salt
freshly ground black pepper

Mix together the tomato dice, purée, basil and 1 × 15 ml spoon/1 tablespoon of the mayonnaise. Fold into the mayonnaise and taste and adjust the seasoning.

Mickeval fish devil; Tomato mayonnaise

Dutch sauce

Metric	Imperial
25 g butter	1 oz butter
25 g flour	1 oz flour
300 ml milk	½ pint milk
salt	salt
freshly ground black pepper	freshly ground black pepper
1 egg yolk	1 egg yolk
1 × 5 ml spoon lemon juice	1 teaspoon lemon juice

Cooking time: about 15 minutes

This is an economical version of hollandaise sauce and is used in the same way.

Melt the butter in a pan, stir in the flour and cook for 1 minute. Remove from the heat and stir in the milk. Return to the heat, bring to the boil, stirring, then simmer for 10 minutes. Add salt and pepper to taste. In a small bowl beat the egg yolk with 1 × 15 ml spoon/1 tablespoon of the sauce, then stir into the pan. Cook over a gentle heat, stirring, until it just comes to the boil. Remove immediately, stir in the lemon juice and taste and adjust the seasoning.

Garlic mayonnaise

Metric	Imperial
1 slice of bread 2 cm thick, crust removed	1 slice of bread ¾ inch thick, crust removed
3 × 15 ml spoons milk	3 tablespoons milk
4 garlic cloves, peeled and crushed	4 garlic cloves, peeled and crushed
2 egg yolks, at room temperature	2 egg yolks, at room temperature
salt	salt
freshly ground black pepper	freshly ground black pepper
300 ml olive oil or salad oil	½ pint olive oil or salad oil
2 × 15 ml spoons lemon juice	2 tablespoons lemon juice

Crumble the bread into a bowl. Pour in the milk and leave to soak for 10 minutes. Squeeze the bread dry. Put into a bowl with the egg yolks, garlic, salt and pepper. Beat well, then add the oil, drop by drop, beating constantly until it begins to thicken, then add the oil faster until it is all incorporated. Stir in lemon juice and taste and adjust the seasoning.

Dutch sauce; Garlic mayonnaise

Tomato butter

Metric
100 g butter
2 × 5 ml spoons tomato
purée
1 × 2.5 ml spoon paprika
1 × 5 ml spoon chopped
fresh basil, or pinch of
dried basil
salt
freshly ground black pepper

Imperial
4 oz butter
2 teaspoons tomato
purée
½ teaspoon paprika
1 teaspoon chopped
fresh basil, or pinch of
dried basil
salt
freshly ground black pepper

Spread on fish and shellfish sandwiches, particularly dressed crab, or serve with all types of grilled and fried fish.

Cream the butter, then work in the tomato purée, paprika and basil. Add salt and pepper to taste. Press into a pot and chill.

Maître d'hôtel butter

Metric
100 g butter
2 × 5 ml spoons finely
chopped parsley
juice of 1 small lemon
salt
freshly ground black pepper

Imperial
4 oz butter
2 teaspoons finely
chopped parsley
juice of 1 small lemon
salt
freshly ground black pepper

Serve with all types of grilled and fried fish.

Cream the butter well. Work in the parsley and lemon juice and salt and pepper to taste. Shape into a roll in greaseproof paper, then twist the ends tightly. Chill. Cut into slices as required.

From left: Maître d'hôtel butter; Roquefort butter; Watercress butter; Tomato butter (behind)

Roquefort butter

Metric	Imperial
50 g butter	2 oz butter
2 × 5 ml spoons chopped fresh parsley	2 teaspoons chopped fresh parsley
freshly ground black pepper	freshly ground black pepper
1 × 5 ml spoon wine vinegar	1 teaspoon wine vinegar
1 × 5 ml spoon made mustard	1 teaspoon made mustard
1 × 5 ml spoon anchovy essence	1 teaspoon anchovy essence
50 g Roquefort cheese	2 oz Roquefort cheese

Serve slices as a garnish on grilled fish, or with hot French bread as an accompaniment.

Cream all the ingredients together until well blended. Shape into a roll in greaseproof paper, then twist the ends tightly. Chill.

Watercress butter

Metric	Imperial
100 g butter	4 oz butter
100 g watercress	4 oz watercress
few drops of anchovy essence	few drops of anchovy essence
salt	salt
freshly ground black pepper	freshly ground black pepper

This goes well with grilled or fried white or oily fish. Alternatively, spread on open or closed sandwiches made with creamed buckling, flaked cooked kipper or cold smoked trout.

Cream the butter well. Chop the watercress leaves and stems very finely, then work into the butter with the anchovy essence. Add salt and pepper to taste. Press into a pot and chill.

Index